paychecks
of the Heart

MARY KAY®

©2000 Mary Kay Inc.

ISBN 1-878096-55-9

First Printing, 2000

Mary Kay Inc.

16251 Dallas Parkway

P.O. Box 799045

Dallas, Texas 75379-9045

U.S.A.

Dedicated to

Mary Kay Ash

Without whom none of us would have known these

"Paychecks of the Heart"

Our promise and commitment to you, Mary Kay, is that we
will always pass the torch you have extended to us.

The Independent National Sales Directors
of Mary Kay

January 2000

Table of Contents

❦

Humor

Compassion and Caring

Family Matters

Business Sensitivity

11

Wisdom

Foreword

I don't believe I've ever known anyone who did not look forward to her paycheck. Money, as we all know, is an important and vital tool for human existence.

However, this book is not about money. Even though my sister National Sales Directors have each earned between $1 million and $7 million in commissions in their careers, all agree there has been a far greater reward to being associated with Mary Kay the woman and Mary Kay the company.

That reward is *Paychecks of the Heart*, those cherished memories and experiences that have given to us much greater meaning, more lasting value and a richer investment than money could ever bring.

It is my hope and prayer that as you read these pages, they will stimulate in you the memories of those times in your life when you have unselfishly reached out to someone. Your act wasn't for strokes, recognition or monetary gain, but from the goodness of your heart and the depth of your soul. Once you've experienced such a "paycheck," your life will be enriched forever.

As we share our stories, we acknowledge this as the ultimate gift of our beloved founder. We do so with love, admiration, pride and respect that words cannot describe.

Rena Tarbet
Independent National Sales Director

Introduction

The folding chairs in the stage left area of the annual Mary Kay Seminar are a hotbed of activity and emotion. This is where stage direction is given, where speakers gather their thoughts before going onstage. It is the staging ground for that first recognition walk beneath the lights and applause that has fueled so many dreams and encouraged so much determination.

Stage left was also the staging ground for this book.

As she awaited her time at the podium, one of the most motivational speakers to ever grace the Mary Kay stage listened intently while a woman onstage shared her life-changing experiences since beginning her Mary Kay business. National Sales Director Rena Tarbet, seated with a Company executive, felt a chill run through her spine.

She and other National Sales Directors had wished for some time to come up with the perfect gift they could give to the Mary Kay Ash Charitable Foundation in honor of their beloved Mary Kay Ash. Something meaningful – not material. Something that would have lasting value and touch hearts. Something money alone could never buy.

"That's it," Rena said. "This is what we can give Mary Kay! We can share our stories in a book! We've got to preserve them. They talk about who we are better than anything."

Tom Whatley knew in an instant what she meant. "You mean like a 'Chicken Soup for the Mary Kay Soul'?" asked the president of U.S. Sales, knowing a gem of an idea when he hears one. The idea, in fact, grew in his heart until this book took shape.

One book could never capture all of the stories – and certainly not even the most dramatic of them. But *Paychecks of the Heart* is a start at capturing one of the most valuable intangibles associated with a Mary Kay career. The stories underscore the real worth of a career lived the way the legendary founder envisioned it. They come as close as anything does to explaining the phenomenal success and more important, the incomparable loyalty so many women have for Mary Kay Ash. All of the women who live their lives today according to her priorities treasure the opportunity to pass this legacy to future generations.

There is space left blank in the book for your own contribution to *Paychecks of the Heart.* Hopefully, you'll be inspired by these pages, add your story, and then share it with us.

prologue:
The Esteemed Emeriti...
Where it all begins

"My objective

was to open doors

of opportunity

to women

that had been

denied me in

the workplace."

The Esteemed Emeriti...
Where It All Begins

These women paved the way
for all the "paychecks"
that were to follow.

As this book went to press, 26 women had ascended to
the revered position of Independent National Sales Director
Emeritus. These are the true pioneers, and their strength is
evident in the motivational role they play today with the
independent sales force.

In the early days they did everything from helping
Mary Kay hang the drapes at the original headquarters

to testing many of the original teaching materials and products. They've "done it all" in the course of their careers, but their most important legacy is the high standards they've established.

Our hats are off in recognition and respect to those who paved the way for all the "paychecks" that were to follow – our NSDs Emeriti:

Margo Andrews, Ila Burgardt, Dee Denison, Anna Ewing, Alma Gaines, Audy Giblin, Sylvelyn Gill, Genevieve Gould, Luella Gunter, Jean Henry, Eddie Howley-Beggrow, Shirley Hutton, Helen McVoy, Idell Moffett, Gerri Nicholson, Lovie Quinn, Sally Rattray, Virginia Robirds, Maxine Sandvig, Carolyn Savage, Mary Jane Schiavone, Karon Strom, Ann Sullivan, Helen Titus, Abbie Webster and Dalene White.

As you will see in the pages to follow, everyone's definition of a "paycheck of the heart" is different. It is colored by their unique life experiences. We asked some of our Emeriti to get us started by defining the phrase for us and others to show us by example. Here is what they said:

The Definition of a "Paycheck"

Ann Sullivan believes the greatest "paycheck of the heart" is that the spirit of Mary Kay Ash lives in the hearts of all those who embrace her Company philosophies. Ann believes this feeling is best portrayed in a favorite saying Mary Kay Ash quotes:

> *"Each of us is an angel with only one wing. We can only fly by embracing each other."*

Through the course of her career, Ann has embraced and been embraced on countless occasions. One memory in particular is etched in her mind. As she lay grievously ill in a hospital bed for 72 days – some of that time on life support – Ann received a telegram from Mary Kay. She kept it under her pillow, and, as she says, "I asked the doctors and nurses to read it lest they ever decided to take me off life support." Ann read the telegram repeatedly throughout her recovery. It said, simply, "You can't leave us. We need you. Love, Mary Kay."

Sylvelyn Gill believes the "paycheck" is the fact that "we succeed by helping other people, and we have the pleasure of watching them grow." Sylvelyn received the greatest paycheck of her career at her Emeritus debut when her daughter said, "My mother never ran her area from her office. She ran it from her heart. Just like Mary Kay."

Sally Rattray likens the "paycheck" to a bountiful garden. "We seed our garden and one day it begins blooming. You harvest friends as well as the income with which you can lead a wonderful life. Mary Kay was correct when she said that in every woman there is a seed of greatness. Those of us with Mary Kay have been fortunate enough to have that seed developed."

Anna Ewing looks back on a career in which she earned "dollars *and* sense." In the big picture, Anna believes the financial rewards of a Mary Kay career are far superceded by "the realization of your abilities - that you can do great things regardless of education, experience or age. The greatest rewards are the encouragement and the principles we were taught to live by. Most incredible to me is the opportunity to pass all this along to others. No deposit in any bank can compare to this kind of investment in the lives of others."

Abbie Webster got a very early "paycheck" under
extremely tragic circumstances. She was one of thousands
attending Seminar in 1974 when word came that her mother
had suffered a heart attack. "I was found in that huge
convention center in just 15 minutes. Mary Kay Ash heard
the news and she left the class she was teaching to be with
me," Abbie recalls. Staff and Sales Director friends stayed by
her side until her family arrived to take her to her mother.
"But just before I left the convention center, Mary Kay gave
me some very good news that wasn't to be announced until
later that day. I had earned the use of my first Cadillac!"

Margo Andrews remembers that the biggest
"paycheck" of her career was when she earned the status
of National Sales Director. People were gathering from
throughout the nation for her celebration, which is
traditionally presided over by one's Senior National Sales
Director. But Helen McVoy's husband was hospitalized, so
a "replacement" was sent. "I was totally surprised to see
Mary Kay herself standing on the stage in San Francisco to
administer my oath. That day I was ever more mindful and
grateful for the rare privilege and responsibility that comes
with being associated with this magnificent Company."

Jean Henry was a single mother who desperately needed to increase her earning potential in 1969. However, in looking back, the things she praises the most are things that money cannot buy. "I feel greatly blessed that my teacher was Mary Kay Ash. Like an artist who is taught everything by the master, the lessons she has instilled in me are so worthy of passing on. Because of Mary Kay, many women have learned how to handle life's disappointments, how to set goals and how to deal with their successes once they achieve their goals." These, says Jean, are the greatest "paychecks" anyone could ever earn.

Helen Titus saw her own personal "paycheck" delivered over a home-cooked meal of Southern fried chicken, potato salad and chocolate pound cake. "Mary Kay was visiting with her husband, Mel, and it was as we sat around my kitchen table breaking bread together that I was reminded how very down-to-earth this woman is. No matter that she's a legend. And something else so small but so revealing of her personality was that after I had shared my recipe, Mary Kay always gave me credit every single time she baked my chocolate pound cake – which was one of Mel's favorites. Imagine how that made me feel."

Genevieve Gould takes great comfort and pride in the memories she has being one of the pioneers in the Boston area. "What fun we had showing Mary Kay our state, eating lobster rolls in a small fisherman's shack and having an elegant lunch at The Ritz. And who could forget taking this legend shopping for boots when she traveled to Montreal one winter without any!"

Gerri Nicholson always appreciated the opportunities provided to her by the Company, but it was after tragedy struck that she realized what Mary Kay really meant when she said this was a caring company. "In 1991, I was driving with my husband when he suffered a heart attack in the car. I cannot tell you how much of a 'paycheck' it was to be in the care not only of Mary Kay, but also the entire sales force and our corporate staff. My husband felt so loved and cared for, and it was then he realized the magnificence of what Mary Kay created."

Samples of a "Paycheck"

Helen McVoy

Direct Deposit to the Heart

By her own estimation, Helen McVoy has touched the lives
of nearly 100,000 women between 1965, when she began
her Mary Kay business, and 1991, when she became an NSD
Emeritus. That "direct deposit" would be paycheck enough,
but Helen says her fondest memory is that of Mary Kay Ash
inspiring her weekly by telling her she was great.

"Her belief in me made me want her to be proud of me,"
says Helen, one of the first two National Sales Directors.
Who wouldn't succeed, she asks, with this kind of
confidence?

"They say it must start at the top. And indeed it did, as
Mary Kay consistently modeled belief, motivation and love.
Yes," says Helen, "some of our paychecks are deposited
temporarily at the bank, but the most significant are
deposited forever in our hearts."

Dalene White

More Than a Cosmetic Change

Her brother had died in the fire that scarred her face. Her neighbor had finally persuaded the woman to come to a skin care class being conducted by Dalene White. Dalene, the very first Beauty Consultant and one of the first two National Sales Directors, treated the woman with tender loving care and sent her off with a pretty new look.

"Three days later, her husband rang my doorbell and asked if he could buy an entire set of products for his wife," Dalene recalls. The man was ecstatic that his wife had finally ventured out of the house – and he was even more thrilled to see how happy she was with her new look.

It wasn't long after that, the woman began to rejoin her community again. She served as president of the parent-teacher association and two years later was elected president of a major women's political organization. Dalene received a call from the husband, who thanked her for "putting my wife on the road to good health again."

Carolyn Savage

One Step at a Time

There is no doubt in Carolyn Savage's mind that Mary Kay is one of the greatest women in history. "She has propelled and inspired more women than any of us can imagine. What is so beautiful to me about her concept is that you achieve success one step at a time. You have somebody up ahead of you who is holding one hand out and pulling you up. There is someone behind you nudging you to move up."

As an early Beauty Consultant, the person holding the hand out for her was Mary Kay Ash. Carolyn learned early that when Mary Kay found out a person had a real weakness, she would cure them of it by asking them to teach that very subject. Mary Kay and Carolyn were driving to Longview, Texas, for Carolyn's first-ever workshop when Mary Kay informed her she would be asked to teach 45 minutes on bookkeeping that day. Carolyn recalls, "I couldn't even balance my checkbook at that time!" Nervous and wringing her hands, she somehow got through the class and determined she would get better at numbers after that experience.

Maxine Sandvig

Priceless

In the rich tapestry of her life, she recalls so many times when Mary Kay "said it all" in just a sentence. Sometimes it was funny. Other times, teasing with a twist of tenderness. Most often, Mary Kay's economy of words touched her heart deeply, as in her first year as a Beauty Consultant.

Maxine had asked her 13-year-old son to entertain at the event Mary Kay was to attend celebrating Maxine's appearance in the Top 10. The occasion was even more special because he had just been released from the hospital after an accident. Mark had a beautiful singing voice, but due to a problem with the lights that night, the pianist wasn't able to play and he had to sing his number unaccompanied.

He thought he'd done a bad job and was so upset, he left the hotel to wait for his mom in the car. When Maxine learned of this, she asked if Mary Kay would carry on the meeting because she was going to see about Mark.

"I'm going with you," said Mary Kay, gathering up her formal gown so that she could walk faster. When Maxine protested,

Mary Kay said, "So you think you can handle something
I can't? Let's go."

Mary Kay put her arms around Mark and they talked as
Maxine watched until he was feeling better. Maxine and
Mary Kay had to go back to their 1,000 guests, but as they
went back into the hotel, she took Maxine's hand, stopped
and the two women knelt to pray that Mark would
overcome his injuries and achieve his full potential. As their
prayer ended, Mary Kay said softly to Maxine, "Come. Our
guests are waiting."

Ila Burgardt

Dragging Main Street

Growing up in poverty, Ila Burgardt was motivated to strive
for success when she was a single mother raising her two
children.

One memory from her school years had haunted her. The
boy who asked her to the junior/senior banquet had to
break the date when his mother protested. "His family was
from the upper social level of that community, and his
mother decided that it wouldn't be proper that he should
escort me."

After she'd seen phenomenal success as a National Sales Director, she and her sister, also a pink Cadillac driver, drove to their hometown in their respective cars. The two girls dragged up and down Main Street of Beaver, Oklahoma, driving and waving from their pink Cadillacs for the entire town to see.

The event stirred up so much attention, the local newspaper covered their drag race as well as the story of their success in full detail. There was one family in Beaver that Ila hoped would read of her success.

They did, and it was one of the best rewards she's ever experienced.

Shirley Hutton

Giving It Away

Shirley Hutton always enjoyed that her "paycheck" paid the bills and afforded her family many things they never would have enjoyed.

Shirley had worked since the age of 11 baby-sitting for 10 cents an hour. She earned 50 cents an hour as a maid for her mother's boss, and at 16, she cleaned other people's diamonds in a jewelry store. She paid her way through college teaching swimming lessons through the Red Cross and working in the university library. She was a secretary, a model and a television anchor before becoming a Beauty Consultant.

"Never in all my life did I ever find any other work where you succeed by giving your career away as in Mary Kay."

Shirley earned a record $7 million in commissions and prizes during her Mary Kay career. She and her daughter, Elizabeth Fitzpatrick, made Company history when they became the first mother-daughter National Sales Director team.

"But the greatest reward is receiving notes from people whose lives I touched in my career. Their thanks have shown me more than anything what Mary Kay means by a 'paycheck of the heart.'"

Karon Strom

Proof in the Pudding

In all the hustle-bustle of a Seminar backstage area, it would be very easy for the caring to get lost in the fray.

Karon Strom got her greatest "paycheck" and the greatest confirmation she'd made the right career decision as she was backstage waiting to go onstage to receive the keys to her first pink Cadillac.

"There was this sobbing woman. Actually, she was hysterical. Mary Kay herself had her arms around the woman and was trying to console her," says Karon. "Mary Kay had tears in her eyes, too."

Karon watched as Mary Kay calmed the woman, gently patting her hand while she gave instructions to several staff members. The Beauty Consultant had lost her purse, which had all her credit cards as well as her airline tickets.

"You could tell that Mary Kay genuinely felt bad about this. Even though there were thousands of people in the arena waiting to see Mary Kay, she wasn't going to leave this woman until someone got help for her."

This, said Karon, told her everything she needed to know.

Idell Moffett

Case Not Closed

After the police stamped "case closed" on an unsolved murder, Idell Moffett decided it was time for the army of angels she knew to take matters into their own hands.

When a Sales Director's daughter disappeared and was still missing 18 months later, Idell made an appointment with a renowned private investigator. His fee was $25,000. Idell got together with some of her friends in the sales force, and they decided to hold a fund-raiser to help raise the money.

As it happened, they didn't need to engage his services because the day after Idell had committed to fund the investigation, the young man suspected of the murder was arrested on another charge.

Idell knew that even though the murderer was in custody, the parents still needed closure about what happened to their daughter, so she negotiated a much smaller fee and did the fund-raiser to pay for the private eye to remain on the case. It paid off.

"The investigator arranged for a cell-mate who would get this man to admit to the unsolved murder and then testify to that," Idell recalls.

Just last year, as the murderer was about to be released from jail after serving 20 years, he was charged and convicted of having a deadly weapon in his jail cell. He was sentenced to prison for an additional 40 years.

"You hear all the time about how people use their earnings to help others. It was because of the Mary Kay career that I was able to help these parents solve this haunting tragedy and come to some finality in this nightmare," says Idell. "God was just waiting for me to take a step."

Eddie Howley-Beggrow

Do You Have a Brother?

Mary Kay Ash had seen Eddie Howley-Beggrow through two
devastating tragedies.

Her son, Michael, had been found killed in a rafting accident
after being lost for 23 days. Her first husband, Pat, had
suffered three grueling years with Lou Gehrig's disease
before he died.

Now that she had become engaged after being widowed for
12 years, the first person Eddie wanted her new fiancé to
meet was Mary Kay. They traveled to Dallas, where they
spent a glorious evening getting to know each other.

As the evening ended, Mary Kay cautioned Bill, "If you
don't take good care of Eddie, she can always come home
to Mama!" And then – as if to signal to Eddie that she
approved – Mary Kay turned her head ever so slightly and
coyly asked Bill, "By the way, do you have a brother?"

Mary Jane Schiavone

Believing is Everything

When she was diagnosed with chronic fatigue syndrome many years before anyone knew about its effects, Mary Jane Schiavone was so concerned about the future of her Mary Kay Beauty Consultants and Sales Directors that she decided the best thing she could do was to quit.

She called Mary Kay, expressing how she didn't feel she had been earning her commission checks and so she would be letting go of her business.

"Nonsense," said Mary Kay. "You think in terms of getting well. You believe you will get well. Believe you will work again. Believing is everything."

Mary Jane continued to explain, but she noticed the phone had suddenly gone dead. She quickly called Mary Kay back. "We were cut off," said Mary Jane.

"No we weren't. You are not quitting. Period." And then Mary Kay hung up again for the second time that day.

"It is very easy to lose yourself when the person in the mirror is not really you," says Mary Jane. "Mary Kay helped me hang on to me."

Mary Jane describes how she was treated with warmth, concern, understanding, kindness and respect by her sister Nationals and the staff. "That kind of treatment allowed me to keep my self-respect in place during some very challenging times," she says.

"Mary Kay is a kind, honest and wholesome role model for all womankind."

Alma Gaines

Mirror Image

One of the things that Alma Gaines always respected the most about her career was that Mary Kay never needed a law or a regulation to mandate how she must treat all people with dignity. Dignity came naturally.

Through one of her Sales Directors, Alma experienced firsthand the sheer joy that came from being able to open the doors of opportunity to a woman who'd battled for acceptance in other careers.

Hazel had a college degree and dreamed of teaching or missionary work. But no one doing the hiring could quite get over the fact that Hazel is a dwarf.

"I have to admit the first time I saw her, I was a little taken aback. But as soon as I visited with her and she told me how hard she had worked for acceptance, I told her I knew she was in the right place.

"Mary Kay is a company where everyone starts out just the same. It doesn't matter your background or your height," Alma told her.

Hazel became a successful Independent Beauty Consultant. She stood on a box to conduct her skin care classes.

Hazel once shared a sentiment that Alma considers the greatest compliment when she said, "Thanks to Mary Kay, when I look in the mirror, I'm just as big as anyone else."

Virginia Robirds

Your Turn to Receive

When she was qualifying to become an Independent Sales Director, Virginia Robirds broke a Company record with the highest wholesale production in one month. As one of the first pink Cadillac drivers in 1969, Virginia's team also would break another record as the unit that had earned the use of the most Cadillacs.

She had spent an entire career building up and helping others.

When her resolve was weakened after the unexpected death of her beloved son, Bill, Virginia found a whole network of her Mary Kay friends who were willing to take over as she grieved. They would help with her meetings and supply her ideas. The same thing happened a few years later when Virginia's late husband, Harold, was diagnosed with lung cancer.

Virginia was telling Mary Kay about all the support she'd received. Mary Kay said something that has remained in her heart as a "paycheck" that had nothing to do with money.

Mary Kay said, "Virginia, you have helped so many for so long. All you send into the lives of others comes back into your life twofold.

"Now it's your turn to receive."

Luella Gunter

Sisterhood

When Luella Gunter begins to balance her checkbook of the heart, there are many vignettes that fill her mind. There is no commission check of any amount that she would trade for the priceless relationships like those she enjoys with women she has met through Mary Kay. Today, many remain closer than sisters.

There is no club membership in the world more valuable than being part of the Mary Kay sisterhood, says Luella. For her, the first clue was at her first Seminar when she arrived a day early and ended up being the only Beauty Consultant in attendance. "I have never felt so accepted as I did that day. Mary Kay's daughter and her friend quickly took me under their wings and made me feel welcome. I sensed a sisterhood I never had before. They really wanted me to have the good life they were enjoying," Luella says.

They were molding the behavior that thousands of Sales Directors would come to follow. "They were preparing me for something great, something that in the man's world where I worked I never knew existed."

Lovie Quinn

One Giant Kiss for Womankind

Having known Mary Kay Ash since before she founded her Company, Lovie Quinn was always certain that following her "dignified and loving" friend would be the path she would follow to security after a divorce left her with five children to raise.

She also was left without a car. Even before they separated, Lovie had limited access to the one family car since her husband traveled all the time. After her divorce she relied on friends to give her rides, or she baby-sat their children in exchange for transportation around Houston as she was building her Mary Kay business.

So it was truly a momentous occasion in 1969 when she became one of the first five Sales Directors to earn the use of a pink Cadillac. Lovie finally had her first car and she had earned it! The photo of her kissing the Cadillac will always and forever be a reminder of Lovie's ultimate "paycheck."

"It was traditional that you greeted Mary Kay first whenever you came onstage. However, that day I sailed right past my lifelong friend and I fell across the car and kissed it passionately." Lovie's kiss caused the car, which had been revolving on an elaborate turnstile, to come to a stop!

In the ensuing years, Lovie has protected and loved her pink Cadillacs with all her heart. So much so that nary a bird dropping has ever touched the luscious pink exteriors.

Dee Denison

Giving and Receiving

It was in honoring a personal request from Mary Kay Ash that Dee Denison gave Mary Kay a wonderful "paycheck," and received one in return.

One day in 1969, Dee got a call from corporate headquarters requesting that she fulfill a request that had been made by Mary Kay. It seems that the founder of Weight Watchers, in Dallas for a speaking engagement, had called Mary Kay saying she wanted to experience a Mary Kay facial.

Dee went to the Fairmont Hotel at the appointed time with her beauty case, where she introduced the products.

That night, Mary Kay and her husband, Mel, were seated on the front row of the State Fair Music Hall where the founder of Weight Watchers spoke. She opened the program by saying: "I will never be fat again. I'll never be a brunette again. And I'll never be without my Mary Kay cosmetics!"

The phone call that Dee received the next morning from Mary Kay Ash was all the "paycheck" she would ever need.

Audy Giblin

The Ones That Got Away

"We touch people in ways we can never imagine," says Audy Giblin of her greatest "paycheck."

Mary Kay Ash often spoke about the many letters she received from people who had discontinued their business for one reason or another. The consistent theme of the letters was always to express gratitude for how much the women had learned and profited – even from a limited exposure to Mary Kay and her principles.

Audy has had the same experience; in fact, she's had it happen twice recently. Once, in the ladies' room of an exquisite hotel in Banff, Canada, Audy was wearing a Mary Kay name badge when a woman introduced herself. "She said that in the two years when she was an Independent Beauty Consultant, she had learned more about the Golden Rule than in all her years growing up. It was really wonderful to have this woman share these feelings with me.

"Her Mary Kay experience also had led the woman to renew her faith, and it was truly humbling for her to thank me for that."

Audy was shopping in her hometown recently when the owner of an ultra-fashionable boutique came over and introduced herself. "I was in your unit many years ago."

The woman thanked Audy for teaching her the business ethics and practices as well as the selling techniques that have made her store so successful. "She told me that our Company had been instrumental in giving her the vision to go after her life's dream."

Inspiration

"*Each of us*

joining hands,

sharing our ideas

and helping

each other

to succeed:

this is the spirit

upon which

our Company

was built."

Asenath Brock

The Vision

There was an angel in the door.
She was dressed in a white
tuxedo shirt embroidered
with pink Cadillacs.

It was the second time Sherry had undergone surgery at St. Paul Hospital in Dallas. She'd been having trouble sleeping, but this day she'd been resting comfortably so her husband decided he could leave for awhile.

He'd only been gone a short while when a vision appeared in her door. She must be dreaming, she thought.

As her husband had left her room and was walking down the hall, he spotted Mary Kay Ash, who was leaving the hospital after routine tests. He walked over to greet Mary Kay and to thank her for calling his wife, Sherry, every Friday for six weeks after she'd undergone her first colon cancer surgery in 1995. Now it was 1997. "Sherry just had a second surgery, and she's in a room down the hall," he said as Mary Kay's assistant wheeled her toward the exit.

The powerful voice Jim remembered so vividly from her phone calls had by then been silenced by a stroke. They shook hands and as Mary Kay was being wheeled to her car, she held onto Jim's hand. He kept walking right beside Mary Kay, delighted for this rare opportunity on the one hand and regretful that his wife Sherry wasn't able to share it.

"He saw Mary Kay pointing backwards as they walked, but her assistant didn't notice," recalls Sherry. Pretty soon they were at the exit door where Mary Kay's car was waiting. She refused to stand up. She pointed decisively back toward where they'd just come from.

"Her eyes were sparkling, and finally she just stomped her foot in the most decisive manner. She flat refused to get into the car. She wanted to visit Sherry and she wasn't taking no for an answer!" says Jim. They went back in.

As Jim got to the door of her room, he shouted, "Sherry, wake up, you've got to see who's here!"

Sherry opened her eyes and there was what she thought must be a vision. An angel with a smile so loving. She rubbed her eyes again. She wasn't dreaming. It was Mary Kay in her doorway.

"There are no words to describe how Sherry felt about that visit from Mary Kay Ash," says Asenath. "I knew as soon as I heard it that it was a priceless and rare 'paycheck' we should share."

Rubye Lee-Mills

The Canvas Awaits Your Brush Strokes

She already had been given the
greatest gift from Mary Kay.
Now she had another one.

Rubye Lee-Mills has spoken hundreds of times since that first occasion when Mary Kay asked her to deliver a prayer. "I'm the one she talks about in her book whose voice was barely audible and who would faint if anyone even looked at me," recalls Rubye with a smile. "Saying I had a bad case of the butterflies isn't quite dramatic enough to explain how shy I was."

Through her unbridled belief in Rubye, Mary Kay cured her of the butterflies and, in so doing, she gave Rubye the self-esteem that she never developed as a young woman. And that would have been enough of a gift.

But by 1971, when the "Lee Peaches" had climbed to the No. 1 position among Mary Kay units, Rubye received another priceless gift. Although she owns magnificent artwork and jewels, this tiny painting remains the most treasured of her earthly treasures.

An original oil painting by Mary Kay Ash. Of butterflies.

The story goes that Mary Kay had taken up painting after she learned that Grandma Moses didn't begin painting until she was in her 70s. Mary Kay tells the story of showing up at an art supply store one day and requesting to purchase "everything I need to become a painter." As the wary clerk packed Mary Kay's trunk with canvases, oils, brushes and other tools of the trade, he muttered something about hoping she knew how to paint.

Well, no, she didn't exactly know how to paint, but she figured she would never know what she could create on canvas unless she tried. After all, she had shown thousands of women how to go about painting the life of their dreams.

A few flowers or some butterflies couldn't be that hard to capture in oil.

Rubye's painting holds a place of honor in her home. Second only to the painting is the note in Mary Kay's handwriting that accompanied it:

Just a little love gift to say thank you for being you!
I wish it were better. I used butterflies because they
remind me of you – exquisite, fragile yet durable!

Mary Cane

Cry in the Shower

*She is a mother of four herself,
but even she cannot imagine
what it would be like to find out that
you've gone from zero to four
children in one day.*

A Sales Director in Mary Cane's area had seen her business take a nose-dive when she had to stop working to spend four days a week at the hospital caring for her ailing mother-in-law. But Mary recalls that even in the face of having to give up her pink Cadillac, Jackie was always positive about the experience – and always certain that her Mary Kay business would bounce back.

Mary had spent time with the Sales Director at the 1998 Seminar, and the two talked about how anxious Jackie was to revive her business.

No sooner did Jackie return home than she was faced with another tragedy even more devastating. Her sister was killed in an automobile accident. Three of her sister's four children were seriously injured.

There was no one to take care of the children. In that one day, Jackie went from having zero children to having four. The three who'd been injured were in three different hospitals with serious injuries that put one in a coma, one on a respirator and one with a brain shunt. Jackie and her husband began the frantic pace of going from one hospital to the other, caring for the children even as they buried her sister and prepared their home for the arrival of four little ones under the age of nine. That included buying everything – including clothing – for them.

"This is when my Mary Kay family went to work," says Jackie. "Our community could not believe all the little things they did for me, like cook for my family, run errands and provide amazing moral support for all of us. People outside Mary Kay commented all the time about how wonderful it is how much our Mary Kay family cares. They began to understand what Mary Kay stands for in a person's life.

"Even in the toughest of times," Jackie recalls, "I had mentors and supporters and caregivers I could call upon." All the care paid off.

All of the children made it home from the hospital, and the one whose injuries were most serious has amazed the doctors who predicted she would never run or jump again. She's not only doing that, she also grew four inches in a year!

As Jackie was reeling from more than 30 weekly therapy appointments necessary for the children's recovery, her Mary Kay family was thinking of other ways to help. Two top Sales Directors organized a drive to establish a college fund for the children.

"During our ordeal, it is the Mary Kay priorities that have made it possible for me to cope: my faith, my family, and the love and support of my Mary Kay career.

"In fact, in my darkest hours I would think to myself, 'What would Mary Kay do?'

"And then I'd remember something I'd heard Mary Kay tell us once. She said that when times were the worst in the early days of her career, she'd try to keep a stiff upper lip in front of the kids. If she needed to cry, she would cry in the shower. In other words, she'd have her downtime when no one else could see."

Jackie's life has changed dramatically, but there is one thing that hasn't changed in all her 15 years with Mary Kay.

"This Company changes your heart. You go from *wondering* what life's about to *knowing* what it's about. You begin to understand where you're supposed to go and what you're supposed to do. I could never have survived this experience without this knowledge and without the support of my Mary Kay family."

Dollie Griffin

Call Us When You Have An Extra $250,000

She had a front-row seat to a miracle.

It was miracle enough that Dollie Griffin had ever connected with Mary Kay in the first place. After she attended her first skin care class, she had to wait eight months for the Independent Beauty Consultant to make a return visit to her remote hometown in Montana. She had to track this Consultant down in Denver to find out how to begin her own Mary Kay business.

Long after she'd become the first Independent Sales Director in Montana, Dollie watched a story unfold in her home state that is, she says, "the only 'paycheck' you'd ever need to have to know this career is lifesaving."

The story involves a Sales Director who had been scheduled for a liver transplant. Every detail was complete – including the plane reservations – when Sandy received word that the transplant could not take place because her health insurance refused to pay for it.

A single mom, Sandy was devastated. She could barely face her two children, ages 11 and 7, with the horrific news.

The day after this happened, Sandy received her weekly *Directors Memo* from the Company in the mail. She wasn't feeling up to reading anything, but one sidebar story caught her eye. The headline read "Organ Transplants" and detailed how Mary Kay Ash was serving as the honorary chair that year for the Children's Organ Transplant Association (COTA).

"There was a line in the story that chilled me to the bone. It said this organization believed that 'no citizen should be denied a transplant because of cost.'" COTA's phone number was in the story.

Sandy picked up the phone and by that afternoon she had been scheduled for an appointment and observation at a transplant clinic. She had a personal phone call from Mary Kay Ash with encouragement aplenty as well as the message, "You must get well for your children." Within the month Sandy had undergone a liver transplant. With Dollie's National Sales Director help, the Mary Kay support network was able, as Sandy recalls, "to absorb all of my worry so that I never had one thought of not making it."

That was in 1994.

Sandy has faced rejection complications twice, but she is healthy today and very proud of the fact that she has been able to maintain her Mary Kay business.

She has only one regret. She has never had the opportunity to thank Mary Kay in person.

"Working my business is how I thank her, and hugging my kids. And feeling normal for the first time in my life."

Freda Addison

Angelic Task

*In her remarks at her NSD debut,
Freda Addison read this poem.*

At the annual angels convention,
The earthling committee did mention,
There's boredom, depression and even repression
In earth woman's current condition!

They're tired of just mopping the floor,
They're locked out of management's door,
They love to be mothers, but given their druthers,
They yearn to do more, more and MORE!

The head angel said, I daresay!
Go find some earth helpers today

Who will echo our call – "Women *Can* Have It All!"
Can you guess whom they found? Mary Kay.

In her dream, Mary Kay saw a vision
Of women in pink on a mission,
Each running her show with a proud, happy glow –
Mary Kay awoke and made a decision.

She dropped everything she was into.
She had one big brainstorm – and then two!
What beauty's about starts inside and flows out.
This career is right for me and for you!

Now women still sweep floors and stairs,
Wipe noses and comfort kids' scares,
But we're dynamite sellers and glamour tip-tellers
Who help others build their careers.

Mary Kay, thanks to you!
You changed your whole life – struggled too!
For an angelic task, you gave all we could ask
To help women's wishes come true.

You've touched so many hearts on your way,
An incredible journey, I'd say!
Your ideas fill pages, your love is contagious.
All angels salute you today.

Mattie Dozier

Hitching Her Wagon

The subject outline she was slated to teach has long since been forgotten.

$\mathcal{M}$attie Dozier had agreed that she'd take time out of her hectic Seminar schedule to teach a group of Consultants attending Seminar. She'd even received a class outline of the kinds of topics she should cover for this class of new Beauty Consultants, many of whom were attending their first Mary Kay event.

Mattie had read a story that moved her, and it started her thinking how she could incorporate the lesson of the red wagon in the story into her class that day. She asked her husband if he would go out and buy a little red wagon. She told him she'd also need some poster board.

"He was bumping his gums all day because he could not find a red wagon anywhere in Dallas. He begrudgingly bought a green suitcase on wheels and asked if it would do!"

As she recalls, she put a lot of effort into preparing for this class. It was about forgetting the past, tearing up all the things that don't matter and concentrating on those that do. She substituted the green suitcase for the red wagon and as she says, "I wheeled that suitcase into the meeting room and began getting rid of everything in it. I was throwing things everywhere and saying 'get rid of all the excess baggage that is dragging you down!' I asked everyone to list their hang-ups on a piece of paper. Then we tore up those papers to symbolize tearing up the things in their past."

The class was a huge hit and Mattie was definitely the star. There was lots of applause, but because of a prior lunch commitment, Mattie had to dash from the class the minute it was over. "I could see the elevator and knew that if I walked real fast I could be the first one on it instead of waiting in a long line! In an instant, I'd have been on that elevator and gone," said Mattie. But something made her pause. She slowed her steps. She looked behind her.

Two women, breathless from chasing Mattie, nearly ran into her as she stopped.

"We just wanted to thank you," one said. Mattie expressed appreciation and began walking toward the elevator again.

"No, wait, you don't understand," said the other woman. "You saved my life in there."

"I appreciate your kindness and am glad I could help," Mattie said.

"You still don't understand. You saved my friend's life," the other one said.

Now they had her attention. Mattie's feet were firmly planted.

The woman told how she had come to Dallas planning to commit suicide at the grassy knoll near where President John F. Kennedy was assassinated. Her friend, sensing her depression, made her agree to attend the morning Seminar classes together. Mattie never learned the woman's name, but she did hear months later that she was working and doing great.

With her topic that day, Mattie had given someone an option. Instead of killing herself, she'd hitched her wagon to a star.

Wanda Janes

The Priorities Live On

She had gone to the meeting
expecting to provide
sympathy to Mary Kay.

*M*ary Kay had just lost her husband, Mel. In that period, Wanda Janes saw a living example of the principles that Mary Kay has so often taught. That she lived them during the time of her greatest grief is a lesson Wanda will never forget.

She had always observed how Mary Kay's daily life was an illustration of her beliefs. When Wanda's husband suffered a near-fatal heart attack, Mary Kay broke through a crowd to personally greet him and celebrate his recovery. When her brother achieved the title of "master craftsman" in the

Knifemaker's Guild, Mary Kay's congratulatory letter made the accomplishment even more special.

"Never was Mary Kay's example more eloquent than when she ministered to Mel as he was dying of cancer. She put everything else on hold and was by his side until the end.

"Her presence made a profound impact on my life. By her actions she showed how a woman of integrity conducts herself even in the midst of heartache. She was there for Mel when she was needed and then when she had done all she could do, she turned to her work.

"As she spoke to her National Sales Directors that night, it was out of the depths of her own grief. She encouraged us, lifted us up and gave us hope to go on and overcome the obstacles, challenges and hurts that would surely come at some point into each of our lives.

"By her example we saw what it means to put God first, family second and career third. I think Mary Kay knew that each of us would experience a loss like this during our lives. It was so important to her that she show us by her example."

Holly Zick

The Paycheck Residuals

*It was more than 20 years ago,
but she can still remember
the look on the woman's face as
she saw the amount she'd
earned her first month as an
Independent Sales Director.*

Sometimes the look on a person's face says it all. Holly Zick saw the look and she understood.

For their very first meeting the woman had spent money she didn't have to buy a new outfit so she would be properly dressed to meet the elegant Mary Kay Sales Director she thought she needed to impress.

"Years later she told me she had spent an extra half hour to make sure her makeup and her hair were perfect. We laughed about the fact that those weren't the things that mattered in being successful with Mary Kay – even though it is a cosmetics company," said Holly.

All Holly remembers is that this attractive woman walked over to her, shook her hand and said, "How do you do. I'm going to be a Sales Director."

She was young and raising her three little girls alone on welfare. The woman worked tirelessly to make a better life for her children.

Holly knew in a handshake this woman would succeed.

Nine months after becoming an Independent Beauty Consultant, she became an Independent Sales Director. She was already on-target for a pink Cadillac the day she opened that $5,000 commission check.

That was followed by a litany of successes that forever changed this woman's life. As Holly watched this unfold, she cherished each moment. The college graduations of her daughters and their fairytale weddings have been residual benefits from that very first check.

"To this day, every time I talk to her I receive a 'paycheck of the heart.' She has never let me forget that I was the one who introduced her to this unparalleled opportunity," says Holly of the woman whose life today has come so far!

Mickey Ivey

She Dreamed of Wearing That Suit

*Mickey Ivey has more than
125 Sales Directors and three spin-off
National Sales Directors in her
area today, but she will always
remember the woman who would
have been her very first
Sales Director.*

"Barbara was Mary Kay through and through," Mickey recalls. She had recently received recognition for suggesting to the Company that *Applause* be the name for the monthly magazine. That name continues to be used today. She had been so excited about becoming a Mary Kay Independent

Sales Director. She had everyone in her family pulling for her and helping her meet her goal. One of the things Barbara was most thrilled about, Mickey recalls, was that she would finally be eligible to wear the prestigious Mary Kay Sales Director suit. That year, it was bright red.

Then the shocking phone call came that Barbara had been killed in a car accident. Her husband, Larry, called Mickey with an unusual request: that his wife be buried in a Sales Director suit. Mickey tried to order a suit, but when there wasn't one available, she didn't hesitate for a minute.

"I picked up my own Sales Director suit from the cleaners, flew to Michigan and handed it to her husband. I told him I would be honored for Barbara to be buried in my suit, and she was."

The widower was deeply touched by this act of kindness. He explained Barbara's dreams and how this Mary Kay business had been a family one. Then he said, "She dreamed of wearing that suit and would have been so pleased to be buried in the Mary Kay suit she had earned but never had a chance to wear."

Mickey stayed in touch with Larry, and years later he remarried. To Mickey's delight, he sold his new wife, Paula, on the career opportunity with the company that had cared so kindly for his late wife. Paula eventually became a Mary Kay Sales Director.

"We never know," says Mickey, "how the seeds that are planted will grow."

Shirley Oppenheimer
God is Going to Use You to Touch So Many Lives

*When she received her
cancer diagnosis, the first
thing she did was to meet
with her priest. The second
thing was to take a call
from Mary Kay Ash.*

What Mary Kay said would come to be the most significant and the most comforting words spoken during her ordeal.

"God is going to use you to touch so many lives," Mary Kay said.

In the ensuing weeks, Shirley continued to receive words of wisdom and encouragement from Mary Kay. Shirley recalls today that she was so wrapped up in what was happening to her that for a long time she never realized that all of this support from Mary Kay was coming at a time when Mary Kay had just suffered the loss of her only daughter, Marylyn. One of the most poignant calls from Mary Kay, in fact, came just two weeks after Marylyn's death.

"Here was this caring and loving mother calling me three times during that month. She always puts herself aside to take care of other people. And having recently experienced great loss herself – she put that aside to make sure I was OK," says Shirley.

The words Mary Kay spoke to Shirley have indeed come true. She believes the greatest blessing of her career has been her ability to pass along to other women what Mary Kay passed along to her. Through her career, Shirley has witnessed so many examples of Mary Kay's reaching out and caring. "This reminds me – and all of us – that we need to continue to carry the torch to reach out with these same kindnesses as Mary Kay has."

Shirley says she is most proud of the example of caring she's been able to provide for her own children. "It has taught my son, Christopher, that entrepreneurs write their own paychecks. And as for my daughter, Terri, this career has given her the opportunity to stay home with her children while they're young – something so many mothers aren't able to do."

Recently, during Terri's childbirth classes, she called her mom, furious at what she'd heard from other young mothers that night.

The instructor had asked each woman in the class to tell what excited her the most about having a baby.

There were all the usual answers, but what cemented for Terri that she'd made the right career choice were the responses of several in answering the question. One woman's answer to what excited her the most about having a baby? "I'll be able to stay at home for six weeks along with having a paid vacation!"

Dianne Velde

"My Fair Lady"

*She'd been beat as she lay
sleeping. Her car had been
used for target practice.*

Throughout her career, Dianne Velde has never felt it
beneath her to speak to anyone about the Mary Kay career
opportunity – especially when a friend asks her to.

"But when this woman came to my home I was a little
amazed. She rode up on a motorcycle wearing cutoff jeans,
barefoot, with her hair pulled back in a rubber band."

Despite her doubts, Dianne proceeded to explain all the
facts of the career.

"She was so full of energy and she so desperately wanted to change her lifestyle that I found talking to her gave me a sense of excitement. I went from wondering why in the world she was at my house to wanting very much for her to give this career a try."

It turns out, Dianne had a lot of work to do. She taught the woman how to sit and how to talk. She practiced with her what to say in certain situations. They had lessons in how to dress, how to style her hair and how to wear makeup.

"She just didn't know how to act in social settings," Dianne recalls. "She was the product of abusive and volatile relationships – both with her parents and in adulthood."

Over time, Dianne watched with pride as the woman blossomed. Because of her career, she was able to escape an abusive relationship. Mary Kay gave her a sense of self-worth she'd never known before.

"The year she made Top 10 in the Consultant Queen's Court of Personal Sales, I can still see her standing on the stage in a beautiful peach evening gown, her hair all done up in long, soft tendrils, with tears flowing down her cheeks," recalls Dianne, who believes she knows exactly how it must have felt for the Dr. Doolittle character in "My Fair Lady" to watch his protégée blossom.

Dianne had the same pleasure, and the greatest thing of all is, it wasn't a play. "It was real life, and she lived happily ever after!"

Eileen Dunlap

Do You Know This Woman?

Margaret was doubtful she'd be able to add a team member based on this kind of lead.

She was an Independent Sales Director-in-qualification with only two more new team members needed to become a Sales Director. She had just gotten off the phone with her Sales Director, Keeta, who lived in Virginia. The two women had been discussing Margaret's predicament.

Only a few minutes had passed when Keeta called Margaret back. It seems the Senior Sales Director had gotten off the phone and picked up a *Guidepost* magazine, where she turned to a story written by a woman from Margaret's hometown in Pennsylvania. Keeta had a feeling that this was no coincidence – she felt she had just been sent a message. But no, she argued with herself, it's too far-fetched to think the author of this story might be interested in the Mary Kay opportunity just because she happens to live in the same hometown as Margaret!

Keeta finally phoned Margaret again and told her of reading the story by the woman who lived in Margaret's hometown. "I was wondering if you know her?" Keeta asked.

Margaret did know her. They'd met socially at the base where both their husbands were stationed. The author's husband was the commander of the base. "Would you call her?" Keeta asked. At first Margaret was hesitant, but Keeta convinced her there could be no harm in calling to comment about the article the woman had written. She respected the advice of her Sales Director, so Margaret called. The two decided to meet for coffee.

At their meeting, Margaret learned that Janet had recently been searching for career options. She loved the idea of becoming an Independent Beauty Consultant. Margaret loved the idea, also, because now she only needed one more person to put her team in place.

A few days later when Janet learned from Margaret that members of the sales force aren't bound by geographic territories, she called her friend in another state, sent her the information and suddenly Margaret had the final number she needed to become a Sales Director.

When these Sales Directors shared their story at one of her area meetings, Eileen Dunlap thought immediately of Mary Kay's comment to the reporter from television's "60 Minutes" program. Morley Safer asked if Mary Kay was using God. Mary Kay looked him squarely in the eye and without hesitating said, "I sincerely hope not. I hope instead that God is using me."

Jo McKean

The Snapshot Says It All

*It is said that one photo is
worth a thousand words.
A thousand "paychecks," too.*

She doesn't even know who took the photograph, but she's always wanted to thank the person. For Jo McKean, this one photo captured it all. Jo doesn't think she could ever do it justice in words, so she's thankful the moment is captured on film.

In July 1993, all her family surrounded Jo as she debuted onstage. As is the case for everyone who experiences it, this occasion is etched permanently in her memory as one of the most special.

Jo doesn't remember what she said that day or the details of what others said about her. What she does recall is the feeling she had as she stood with two of her grandsons as her two favorite women in the whole world had a little argument!

It was a moment the family talked about for years; one that Jo herself will never forget, although she's shy about recalling it lest she sound the least bit conceited.

"My mom was thanking Mary Kay for all that she had done for me. Mary Kay was thanking my mother for having such a wonderful daughter. They were arguing who was the most appreciative."

The photo captures all the emotions of decades of dreams and hopes as these two positive and influential role models spar over who's the most grateful for Jo!

It is one of those Norman Rockwell-type honest portrayals of emotions that simply cannot be captured in words. Jo doesn't know whether it was her mom's influence or Mary Kay's that was so instrumental to her success. All she knows is that it has been a life blessed beyond belief. Thank goodness for the portrait of that priceless opportunity.

Darlene Berggren

Making a Life

*There's a personal touch that
is often the difference
between earning a living
and making a life.*

*F*ortunately for her, Darlene Berggren saw it early enough in her career that it made a huge impression. One day of examples was enough to convince Darlene that most of the time success is defined in little things: the daily examples.

In 1980, she was in the new Sales Director class that was the largest ever at that point in the Company's history. It was also the December following Mary Kay's loss of her dear husband, Mel.

Some worried if Mary Kay would feel up to hosting this crowd. They even wondered if they'd be allowed to continue the tradition of having their photo made in Mary Kay's famous pink bathtub. Everyone assumed the tradition of Mary Kay baking the cookies herself; brewing her special tea or decorating her home would be dispensed with this year.

Staff did try to make some changes – like having one group photo instead of individual shots. But Mary Kay posed for a personal picture with each of the women – a process that took hours.

"I've always said that if I were ever the one people were waiting in line to meet, I would do everything in my power to make that meeting special for them," she said. "Because once I *was* the person at the back of the line."

She did bake, make tea and decorate. Copies of her recipes were sent home with the new Sales Directors as usual.

And by the time she'd returned home, Darlene saw that her husband had even received his own thank-you letter from

Mary Kay. "She told him she appreciated all he had to do the week I was gone."

That was the day, Darlene says, she decided this was the life, not just the living, she wanted to make.

Jan Harris

"She Has A Good Representative In You"

*Jan Harris had always been
taught to pretend as if
Mary Kay Ash herself were
attending her skin care class.*

$\mathcal{T}$his one particular class had a woman in attendance who was every Beauty Consultant's nightmare. She was rude, unkind and unfriendly. She said she didn't like the techniques as Jan had explained them. She wanted to stay late and have her makeup redone after everyone else had left. Jan just wanted to go home.

"I kept telling myself that Mary Kay says it's not about profit and loss, it's about people and love. I had conducted myself as if Mary Kay were there and so I was very kind," Jan recalls. She stayed late and helped the woman re-do the makeup.

"My intention wasn't to be kind to her because I wanted to, it was because we represent Mary Kay cosmetics."

Two days later the woman called Jan. "Thank you for being kind to me when I was so rude," she said. She explained to Jan that she was terminally ill and that when someone had complimented her on her makeup at bingo, she suddenly knew she needed to call Jan and thank her.

"Tell your Mary Kay that she has a good representative in you."

Jan never saw the woman again. But she continues to conduct every class as if Mary Kay is seated right beside her.

Humor

&

"Humor helps

us put

difficulties

in the proper

perspective,

so that

we don't

take ourselves

too seriously."

Doretha Dingler

Laughing All the Way

Her ranking at the top of the
independent sales force
has afforded her nothing if not
a front row seat for all
the merriment created by the
inimitable Mary Kay Ash.

"All those years appearing at official functions together, I was the one doubled over laughing while Mary Kay was sitting at the head table looking angelic," says Doretha Dingler. "No one but those seated right next to her could hear her hilarious comments. I must have looked so ridiculous! She would say something so funny, but she'd only say it loud enough for those of us seated next to her to hear."

Doretha fondly recalls the one time that Mary Kay couldn't contain her humor – the time when Mary Kay's own peals of laughter and tears spilled over into an entire meeting room and literally giggled the meeting to a halt.

It was the first time Mary Kay's Independent National Sales Directors had gathered at a resort for such a meeting – which is renowned for its jet-set destinations (Monte Carlo, Banff, Hawaii) – where the elite celebrate their success.

But this first location was anything but posh. It was held at a resort better known for its hunting lodge atmosphere than for its plush decor. By the time her private plane had landed, Mary Kay began sensing that her desire for a glamorous locale to honor her top saleswomen was, in fact, just the opposite.

It seems that the connecting airport to the resort was also the means by which the state transferred convicts – most of whom were chained to their seats for the plane ride with the National Sales Directors of Mary Kay decked out in all their finery.

The first morning of the conference, Mary Kay arrived at the meeting room to hear tales of rooms so remote many of the

Nationals had to call the resort's management to guide them to the conference rooms.

Once the meetings began, they were contemplating serious Company business when, as Doretha recalls, Mary Kay started laughing so hard that her shoulders were shaking and tears were rolling down her face.

The laughter caused the speaker to stop talking. All eyes were on Mary Kay. She couldn't manage to get a word out for laughing.

Finally Mary Kay pointed to the ceiling and its exposed water pipes.

By the time she composed herself enough to speak, the entire roomful of the most successful Mary Kay sales force members had figured it out and were laughing right along with the founder.

Mary Kay said, "We really know how to motivate you to greatness, don't we? Riding with convicts chained to their seats, having to call a hunting guide to find the meeting room, and finding exposed pipes where the chandeliers are supposed to be."

Doretha wasn't the only one laughing that day. The message of finding humor when the situation seems bleak came across to everyone in the room.

"She's always had a way of finding the bright side, and of learning through laughter. These are lessons I'll never forget," says Doretha.

Wanda Dalby

Do It Anyway

It was a battle of two stubborn wits. Thirty seconds seemed like 30 minutes.

$\mathcal{W}$anda Dalby's hand was being so firmly held by Mary Kay Ash that she knew she dare not let go. What had precipitated this "standoff" was a comment Wanda made as a photographer was preparing to take her photo with the Company founder.

"I hate to have my picture taken."

This camera shyness had started in her childhood when Wanda, the youngest of nine, was constantly teased by her family – especially by her six brothers. She was so shy that she developed a complex that lasted well into adulthood, motherhood, and even into her career success of earning the use of her first pink Cadillac.

The Cadillac was how she happened to be standing with Mary Kay for a photo opportunity.

Mary Kay signaled the photographer to back off. With hundreds of Cadillac drivers waiting to have their photo taken with Mary Kay, she stopped everything and took Wanda to a quiet corner.

"What did you say?" Mary Kay asked.

"Oh, Mary Kay, it's no big deal. I'm not photogenic, so I hate to have my picture taken," Wanda replied.

"I want you to do something for me, Wanda. Every time you face a camera, I want you to use positive self-talk and say the words, 'I love to have my picture taken.' Will you do that for me?"

This moment seemed to stretch into eternity.

Wanda wasn't about to lie to Mary Kay Ash, so she couldn't manage to utter those words.

And Mary Kay wasn't about to let go of Wanda's hand until she'd heard them.

Mary Kay persisted. "Every time you have your picture taken, you say it." And then Mary Kay reminded Wanda of the biblical passage, "what a man thinks, he becomes."

Wanda still gets tearful as she recalls that day two decades ago. "My hands were shaking. My eyes were misting. I couldn't utter those words. And Mary Kay was not about to let go of my hand."

In this contest of wits, Mary Kay won. Wanda finally managed to mumble the words Mary Kay wanted to hear.

"I'll say, 'it's my job to like having my picture made.'"

And with that, the photo session commenced. Wanda Dalby had been forced in a sweet and precious way to face what had been a lifelong hang-up.

"I still don't like to have my picture made, but from that moment until today I say, 'it's my job to like having my picture made,'" Wanda says.

Thanks to Mary Kay's persistence, the poised and confident Wanda understands that photos come with the position. People who knew her back then, in fact, still cannot believe that was Wanda Dalby smiling broadly and glamorously at them from the cover of a recent Company brochure!

Joan Chadbourn

Upstaging Mary Kay

She only took her eyes off her
3-year-old for a few seconds,
but in that instant he had
worked his way right next to
Mary Kay Ash, who was speaking.

oan Chadbourn, like every mother, wanted to be surrounded by her loved ones during the monumental moment when she would be named National Sales Director. So she decided that Tara, 5, and Philip, 3, would join her and her husband onstage.

It is, after all, a Mary Kay custom, she reasoned, and surely they will be entertained enough by the Dallas Convention

Center stage, the bright lights and the 8,000 cheering people in the audience that they won't get into too much mischief.

It was all downhill from there.

Joan's first challenge as she basked in the glow of recognition was to keep Philip from disrobing. He'd gotten so warm that he began taking off his jacket, his short trousers and knee socks right there on the stage.

Then he and Tara discovered all the shiny, sparkling sequins on the stage (evening gowns do shed)! And they began doing what kids normally do – stuffing them in their noses and eating them as the audience roared!

But that wasn't enough. When Mary Kay began speaking, Joan allowed herself to lose sight of Philip for a few seconds. By then, he had worked his way over to the spotlight where Mary Kay was speaking and he began turning somersaults.

"Philip is probably the only person to ever upstage Mary Kay Ash," laughs Joan today.

Noticing the child, Mary Kay turned and, in her typical quick-witted style, very calmly said, "Philip, I bet you thought I just came in a jar."

The audience went wild. Philip suddenly got very still.

And Mary Kay resumed her remarks.

Carolyn Ward

If They Could See Us Now

*She has shared many fond memories,
but her favorite is the night she
learned just how down-to-earth and
fun-loving her mentor could be.*

 $\mathscr{M}$ ary Kay had been the guest of honor at a formal
event held at a luxurious hotel in the French Quarter of
New Orleans. "She was so lovely and glamorous. And the
crowd was not only in awe of her in her beautiful black
evening gown and sparkling diamonds, but also her words
of wisdom and encouragement," recalls Carolyn Ward.

After the event, Mary Kay had stood for hours signing
autographs and posing for photos with everyone who

wanted one. She always believed that when you are the privileged one everyone wants to meet, you should treat everyone – no matter how long the line – as if they have a sign around their neck that says "make me feel important." And that's exactly what Mary Kay did that night.

By the time the last guest left, Mary Kay had been standing for hours. Her feet were swollen, but nonetheless she wanted Carolyn and her husband, Larry, to walk with her to her hotel two blocks away.

It was very late and there were not many folks on the street. Carolyn says, "As soon as Mary Kay hit the street, she whipped off her shoes and walked through the French Quarter in her stocking feet."

When they got to the corner, Mary Kay spied a hot dog vendor just closing up his cart. She announced that she just had to have one of those hot dogs.

"I should have known," says Carolyn, "since hot dogs and cheeseburgers are two of her favorite foods!"

"So there we were with the one and only Mary Kay, with her shoes tucked under her arm, standing there on Bourbon

Street in all her elegance eating a hot dog filled with chili, cheese and onions! That sight made Mary Kay more real and precious to me than anything in the world. I will forever hold that picture in my heart."

María Elena Alvarez

The Real Person Behind the Name

*Long ago before news was
transmitted instantly around the
world, they made a pact on
the plane. If any media were
to show up, she was to
pretend she was Mary Kay.*

Something about the chemistry between Mary Kay Ash and María Elena Alvarez ensures that whenever the two are together, there is going to be something hilarious going on.

"She is such a real person," María says of Mary Kay. "She makes you feel comfortable with who you are.

"She never pretends to be somebody she's not."

Well, except for once.

María Elena was accompanying Mary Kay Ash to Argentina. She met Mary Kay at the Miami airport dressed in her finest suit and full-length fur.

"Mary Kay made me promise that since I was dressed 'to the nines' and she wasn't, that upon our arrival if there were any Argentine media waiting, I was to pretend I was Mary Kay!"

Cuban-born María Elena speaks with a lilting Spanish accent and has dark hair! "I worried the entire plane trip that I would have to make-believe I was Mary Kay," María recalls.

Then there was the time María Elena was hosting Mary Kay at a dinner in her home in Puerto Rico. María Elena wanted everything to be extra special, so she asked a Norwegian baker to create a very special dessert.

María Elena even told Mary Kay to save room for the dessert.

As dinner preparations were concluding, Maria Elena received word from the baker that there had been an emergency and the dessert wasn't coming. Frantic, she pleaded with her next-door neighbor for a solution.

"All she had was a Sara Lee pound cake, which I borrowed and scurried home to decorate myself," recalls María Elena.

When the dinner was over, Mary Kay asked for the dessert recipe!

"I had to tell her the truth," says María Elena, and this gave them both cause for a good laugh. Then, Mary Kay was reminded of the time she'd had her own kitchen disaster.

Mary Kay explained how she was hosting a tea for groups that arrived at her home at staggered times. Midway through the event, her dishwasher malfunctioned, and with no time to hand-wash the china and no place else to store the dirty cups and plates before the next group arrived, "I instructed the kitchen staff to stash them in the pool."

Which they did just as the doorbell was ringing to signal the next group's arrival.

Rita Potter

When in France

Since arriving in Paris, the top
Sales Director group had enjoyed many
extravagant gourmet French meals.
Mary Kay was craving a
bowl of French onion soup.

Rita Potter was among a small group that heard Mary Kay's plea for soup and sought out the name of a quaint little outdoor café where onion soup and French bread were specialties. On one of their last days when the agenda was free, the group set out for the café. It was a picture-perfect day, and everyone was in the mood to savor the beautiful setting as well as the company of their idol.

"We all ordered – you guessed it – French onion soup and French bread," says Rita.

"What we didn't count on was that dozens of American tourists and other people would recognize our first lady. Everyone told her they had read about her, seen her on television, or they had a friend or family member who was a Beauty Consultant!"

As always, Mary Kay was her usual genuinely gracious self, taking time out to visit and listen to each person. There were still people waiting to speak to Mary Kay when the car arrived to take the Sales Directors and Mary Kay back to the hotel.

Mary Kay's soup and bread were sitting there, cold and untouched, and she never uttered one word of protest.

"In the car, Mary Kay told us that it was more important to make these people feel special than to eat her soup! She said she hoped we'd all have acted the same way if we were ever in that situation."

Anita Bertalot

Incognito

*Everyone thinks they'd relish
being famous, but it certainly
prevents you from going
on any covert shopping trips.*

Anita Bertalot and Mary Kay thought they were being
very discreet when they skipped lunch at a top Sales
Director meeting in Hong Kong to go shopping at an
outdoor market.

They managed to sneak out of the hotel, but at the bazaar
Anita noticed that many shoppers were recognizing Mary Kay.
One woman from Canada and another from China were the
only two who actually approached the pair as they shopped.

"Are you THE Mary Kay?"

"Are you the REAL Mary Kay?"

Mary Kay nodded yes and went on about her shopping. She was thrilled with the vast array of merchandise and the bargain prices, Anita recalls. "I, on the other hand, was just so thrilled to be in the company of this great lady. I couldn't believe that people recognized Mary Kay halfway around the world long before we established our international business. But watching how she handled all the attention gave me an even greater sense of awe."

Anita and Mary Kay both liked the same pair of silk evening trousers. When she realized Mary Kay was planning to buy them, Anita thought it might be better not to purchase a pair for herself. But Mary Kay urged her to purchase the identical item, assuring Anita it wouldn't bother her in the least if they both wore them at the same event.

"She is just so normal," says Anita. "Just like your best girlfriend until you realize WHO she really is and what a legacy she has created for all women."

Cheryl Warfield

People Sense

*How could she have known that
the very spot she had picked
to meet 25 of her area members
was the exact place that Mary Kay
had retreated to relax?*

*P*eople have waited in long lines for hours on end to meet Mary Kay. The last thing Cheryl Warfield would contemplate is for Mary Kay to have to meet and greet any more people following the close of a big event like Seminar.

It was the end of an exhilarating but exhausting three days – the first of five Seminar groups to gather in Dallas. "We were all exhausted. Our feet hurt from walking on the concrete floors in heels. I was even questioning the wisdom of having made plans to meet people for lunch. But I was glad we had decided to wait out the crowds exiting the Dallas Convention Center by gathering backstage in the hospitality room. There were 25 of us going to lunch," recalls Cheryl.

As she rounded the door to the now-deserted hospitality room, Cheryl spied Mary Kay walking into that very room. She knew Mary Kay must be at least as exhausted as everyone else was, so Cheryl stopped at the door to prevent anyone else from entering.

"Mary Kay saw me blocking the door. She wanted to know what was going on. I went in and very sheepishly told her that we would wait in the hallway so we wouldn't disturb her."

"Nonsense," Mary Kay told Cheryl. "Come on in so you can rest your feet while you wait for the others to arrive."

Cheryl went to the hall and asked everyone to please go in the other door, take a chair and sit quietly. "And don't bother Mary Kay! She's got to be tired!"

After watching everyone quietly file in and sit down, Mary Kay smiled broadly. She stood up, walked over and sat down right in the middle of the group. She started telling stories and the best jokes she'd heard at Seminar. She even invited anyone with a camera to take pictures.

Cheryl respectfully protested, "But, Mary Kay, you must be so tired. And you've got four more Seminars to do."

"Nonsense," said Mary Kay. "I get my energy from being with my sales force. Let's do more pictures!"

"That energized me," says Cheryl. "Putting others ahead of ourselves; making others feel important in spite of how tired we might feel at that moment. I saw, in action, the key to Mary Kay's tremendous energy and her strength. Every day I try to live up to that example."

Karlee Isenhart

The 15-Minute Miracle

It was 15 minutes until closing and the distribution center was 300 miles away. She knew she had to work a miracle.

One of Karlee Isenhart's Independent Beauty Consultants, Connie, had been working very hard at her business and was ready to place the order that would mean she qualified to drive a career car.

It would, however, have to be entered by close of business on that last day of the month.

Karlee was frantic, but at the same time she was heartened to think that this woman believed so strongly in her abilities. "She must have somehow thought that in 15 minutes I could get an order to a distribution center 300 miles away. This was in the days before computer and telephone ordering!"

Not wanting to let Connie down with realism, Karlee called the Mary Kay Distribution Center and asked to speak to "any Sales Director in the lobby."

"An angel came to the phone," recalls Karlee. "She didn't even know me, but she took this long order over the phone and then wrote a personal check to pay for it before they closed. All she had was my word that I would mail her a check."

Karlee mailed the check the next day and promptly left on a business trip. While she was gone, the check she'd sent to the "angel" bounced.

Upon her return home, there was a polite and understanding phone message from the woman who was still out her money. They worked it out with no hard feelings.

"Where else but Mary Kay?" asks Karlee. Where else would someone like that come along to help just when she was needed the most? Connie, by the way, has now achieved the Sales Director Half-Million-Dollar Circle of Achievement.

Karlee adds, "And Connie still believes that miracles can happen at the last minute every month!"

Judy Newton

The Shirt Off My Back

*Judy Newton was one of the
U.S. sales force members attending
the Canadian Seminar that year.
She noticed Mary Kay looking
at her in an unusual way.*

"I wondered if my slip was showing, or something like that, but then I just dismissed the thought," recalls Judy.

Later that same day, Mary Kay and Judy were posing for a photograph when Mary Kay let Judy know it was her elephant necklace she'd been staring at earlier.

Mary Kay said, "It's that necklace. It's so gorgeous. And you know, I'm speaking to the National Republican Women's Conference. Wouldn't it be perfect if I wore your necklace?"

Judy says, "I would gladly have ripped off my necklace – or anything else I was wearing – and given it with joy to Mary Kay, but she wouldn't have it. She took me by the hand and we went over to her security guard.

"As if I wouldn't trust her, Mary Kay said, 'You can trust him with the necklace.'"

Judy never expected to see her necklace again, thinking Mary Kay would forget whose it was. And that would have been fine with Judy. She'd always have the memory of giving Mary Kay the necklace off her neck!

Two weeks later, in a box Mary Kay had wrapped herself, the necklace arrived with a personal note of thanks for the loan.

Judy laughs about her misjudgment. As with so many of Mary Kay's actions, there was a lesson to be learned. "No matter how important you are or how busy you become, always be a woman of your word."

"Mary Kay taught us to be that kind of woman. My necklace is just an example that she is, above all else, that kind of woman herself."

Marilyn Welle-Villella

My, What Great Taste You Have

*What is the worst faux pas
a woman attending
a formal event can commit?*

She can show up at the gala wearing the identical outfit as the hostess.

Which is exactly what Marilyn Welle-Villella did the very first year she was a Top 10 Sales Director. She was standing in the wings waiting for her name to be called to walk onstage at Awards Night when she spotted Mary Kay Ash wearing the identical gown to hers.

Marilyn recalls, "I immediately thought about rushing back to the hotel to change, but then I remembered that I'd have nothing to change into. This was the only formal I owned! Anyone I might borrow a gown from was already seated in the arena!"

As she heard her name called, knowing she could avoid her fate no longer, Marilyn sheepishly walked up to Mary Kay on the stage to receive congratulations.

"I'm so sorry, Mary Kay. I am just horrified," Marilyn whispered.

Mary Kay replied, "Don't be, Marilyn. I was just thinking what great taste you have!

"I love the fact that we're dressed exactly alike. I guess the designer didn't realize we'd both be wearing this to the same event. Let's get our photo made before the night is over."

Marilyn walked across the stage. Actually, floated is more like it.

She never had the courage to tell Mary Kay that she hadn't gone to a designer for the dress. "Knowing how she loves a bargain, I didn't have the nerve to tell her I'd bought mine off the rack on sale in Minneapolis!"

Barbara Sunden

The Gift

This "paycheck" about her actual
paycheck stemmed from applying the
Golden Rule to a special Christmas gift.

It was two weeks before Christmas, and she was trying to think of something very special that she could do for her husband this particular holiday. Suddenly, Barbara Sunden had a vision.

She was reminiscing about how very supportive Rich had always been of her career and her success. How he'd been there standing behind her, encouraging her as Barbara built a Mary Kay business that had brought her many, many rewards.

"I remembered particularly how special, how validated I felt each time I earned the use of a new pink Cadillac every two years since 1976. And with every new success, Rich would be there applauding and smiling," Barbara says. "He was always so happy to see me achieve my dreams."

Wouldn't it be nice, she thought, to use her Mary Kay earnings as well as Mary Kay's teachings about the Golden Rule to thank her husband for always being there to cheer her on? To give him a gift that would allow him to experience that same sense of elation she'd felt with every new car?

"Mary Kay had always believed in providing gifts for us that we would never buy for ourselves. I knew instantly the perfect gift to buy for my husband."

Although he'd never said anything about it, Barbara remembered one car that her husband especially liked at the auto show they'd recently been to.

"I called the dealership and described the car he had sat in. They were able to locate the exact car for me."

Due to Barbara's hectic schedule, she let the dealer know all the details would need to be completed by telephone and before Christmas. The dealership took all the financing information by phone and Barbara wired them the deposit money.

A few days later, Barbara was shocked when she learned that she'd been declined for the financing.

Why?

"Well, Mrs. Sunden," said the saleswoman, "you're buying a $60,000 car and you only earn $29,000 a year."

Barbara paused, realizing instantly what had happened. "Please take the paperwork out again. I think you read it incorrectly," she said. "That was a month – $29,000 a month."

The financing was not only approved, the dealer delivered the car complete with a bow.

Emily McLaughlin

Life's Little Instructions

In the early days, someone thought
it would be a wonderful idea
to have a pink Cadillac
pull a pink plow guided
by Mary Kay Ash for a symbolic
groundbreaking celebration.

When she was asked to participate in the ceremony to open the Northeast Distribution Center, Emily McLaughlin had no idea what it was she had agreed to.

"I'd never driven a Cadillac before," says Emily. "Least of all one hitched to the plow that was guided by our Company founder!"

When the day dawned, several days of rain had left the
ground saturated with water. There was mud everywhere.
Emily's greatest fear was that she would drag Mary Kay
through the mud or splatter mud all over her!

Emily was so distraught she sought out Mary Kay and shared
her fears. Mary Kay had some very meaningful instructions –
words that were as much about how to achieve success in
business as they were about successfully pulling the plow.

"You know, Emily, that Cadillac will drive by itself if you just
let it. All you need to do when you're ready to go is just put
the car in gear, take your foot off the brakes, and gently give
the pedal a little gas."

Emily did just as Mary Kay suggested, and she pulled off
the stunt with neither a hitch nor a splatter in sight.

Later on, as Emily thought about Mary Kay's instructions,
she realized the double meaning – what Mary Kay really
intended for Emily to understand.

There is great power to be unleashed inside each of us
when we put our minds in gear, take the brakes off

our thinking and stop limiting our options. And, finally, to press on the gas to add our energy and enthusiasm.

Compassion and Caring

❧

"Those things

which you believe

with your heart,

speak with

your mouth and

act out in love

will inevitably

come to pass."

Gwen Sherman

4 Mom

The seeds that were planted
many years ago
continue to bear fruit.

There are many mother-daughter teams working in the Mary Kay career today. Sometimes it's the mother who encourages the daughter and vice versa.

Gwen Sherman has watched one family use the Mary Kay opportunity to combat their tremendous loss, to find their strength and their grounding, along with the courage to face overwhelming grief. Amazingly, this teamwork continues despite the fact that the mother is now deceased.

Chris had recruited her mom years ago. Wanting to earn the use of a car motivated Chris in the beginning. Chris' career wavered, but her mom, Joan, became the one really committed to her career. Even when Joan suffered a brain aneurysm and lay in a coma for months, her family knew that she would want them to continue ordering product and servicing her customers. They did this with Gwen's help.

"I'll never forget that husband's phone call. He totally trusted me with deciding what he should order to have on hand for a special event they were going to proceed with."

With his daughter's help, the husband held the traditional Mary Kay holiday open house in his wife's absence. The now-comatose woman had always loved the event, and this one had been scheduled prior to her illness. Joan's sister Beauty Consultants pitched in to help, with the tremendous support of Chris' adopted Sales Director, Esther.

True to form, Joan's first request when she came out of the coma was for her Mary Kay datebook! "She had been a Star Consultant 49 times and wasn't about to let illness stop her streak," says Gwen. By the time she was released from the hospital, her family had created a bedroom office where Joan could work her business from her hospital bed.

Because the room tended to be cold, and she was bedridden, they even built a fireplace to keep her warm.

In the last months of her mother's life, Chris saw all the good that had surrounded the family because of her mother's love for Mary Kay. As a result, she re-joined the Company.

"For me to see the seeds planted and how they are now beginning to bear fruit out of this woman's loss has been such an overwhelming feeling. This particular family demonstrated once again how much a company can be like a family," says Gwen.

Recently, when Chris was one of the Top 5 in Gwen's group, she decided to give her entire family a ribbon – from her father to her 6-year-old niece. They had all worked together to make this happen. Chris continues to progress, earning No. 1 in sales in Gwen's unit in 1999.

Chris recently held her first open house since her mom died, and she had $2,300 in sales.

As for earning the use of a car – her original motivation – Chris is working on that goal now. She has, in fact, already selected the personalized license plates, which read: 4 Mom.

Mollye Morrow

The Only Yellow Foundation

She is one who saves everything,
but it's a tube of yellow foundation
that's her most prized memory.

ollye Morrow never wore much makeup. "I never even learned how to apply eyeliner until after I became a National Sales Director," says Mollye, who still refuses to wear nail polish.

She is by her own description a polar opposite of her dear friend and mentor, Mary Kay Ash.

"I'm rambunctious; she's ladylike. She's short and blonde; I'm tall and dark-headed. Mary Kay is soft. I'm what you might call outrageous," says the outspoken Mollye, who lives in a log cabin in the mountains with her engineer-turned-preacher husband.

Her Mary Kay career has seen Mollye and her family through all kinds of things, including some very dark days when Mollye was struck with valley fever that spread into her entire system. Her medicines had to be fed through an intravenous tube, and there was a long needle inserted into the back of her head for a time. Mollye overcame brain surgery, being in a coma and knowing her husband had been told she would probably not survive. She also had to learn to walk, talk, write and speak again.

On one of her first trips following her two-year battle, Mollye was with Mary Kay at a Company event. "Everyone was oohing and aahing over the latest prototype of a new product – the classic yellow *Day Radiance*® foundation. Mary Kay had talked her scientists into letting her have a sample and, of course, we all wanted it. But Mary Kay said she couldn't let anybody have it because it was the only one. And besides, she needed it herself!"

Later that day, Mary Kay motioned for Mollye to follow her into the powder room.

"As a result of my illness, I had blemishes all over my face. Mary Kay took out the priceless yellow product and she gave it to me. She said I needed it more than she did."

Mollye kept that container for years after it was emptied. To Mollye, it became a symbol of the larger purpose of the Company as seen through the eyes of its founder. "Mary Kay dreamed of helping women, whether that meant creating a business opportunity that would allow them to be at home with their children – which she did for me – or, whether it meant creating a product that would help a woman feel better on the outside. I cannot tell you how much better I felt on the 'inside' – and on the outside – after Mary Kay shared with me her only tube of yellow *Day Radiance* foundation."

Arlene Lenarz

Wrapped In a Warm Blanket of Love

*She sponsored a contest
that no one wanted to win.*

*A*rlene Lenarz has read all the books about how you motivate people. She studied at the feet of Mary Kay Ash and learned how to reach out to care for others. She understands that compassion springs straight from the heart.

As the No. 1 National Sales Director in all of Mary Kay for several years running, Arlene has achieved every success imaginable.

Yet her greatest gift has nothing to do with money. It came when a group of Sales Directors in her area galvanized all of their strength and all of their love to wrap one of their own in a warm blanket of love.

"With no guidebook, they did exactly as Mary Kay would have done. We old-timers wonder sometimes if the new generations get it. These women certainly do," says Arlene.

Cheryl was one of the most beloved Sales Directors Arlene had ever met. When a terrible cough didn't go away, and after bronchitis and pneumonia robbed her of her strength, the terrible diagnosis of cancer did nothing to dampen her spirit or her love for her Mary Kay career.

She went through a three-year ordeal with cancer, and every step of the way one of her sister Sales Directors walked with her. One of them drove her for every visit to the hospital. They called her customers to service their needs when Cheryl was too sick. They held sales meetings in her behalf and taught classes to her unit members. There were meals cooked and served on a daily basis.

An angel fund was established to pay for the little necessities Cheryl would never ask for.

The group even worked with Cheryl's husband to plan what would be her last birthday party. When they asked Cheryl what gift she wanted, she said she'd like a conversation with Mary Kay.

Arlene made Mary Kay aware of this wish, and Mary Kay left an event to call Cheryl right in the middle of her birthday party.

But there was one other surprise. It had already been decided by her Sales Directors that the winner of the prize in the contest that Arlene annually runs within her area was – unbeknownst to Cheryl or Arlene – to be given to Cheryl and her husband. It was a four-day beach condo vacation.

"The spirit of giving is so evident throughout this Company. I would have to say that, as unusually heartwarming as this story is, it is one of many that could be shared," says Arlene.

"I've never seen so much love and so much Mary Kay spirit as was captured in Cheryl's story.

"Nothing makes me prouder."

Ronda Ulrich

Up From the Depths

*The woman was a battered wife
on welfare, working three jobs
and raising six children alone.*

She had expressed an interest in earning some extra money to buy Christmas presents for her children.

No one knew when Kathy attended Ronda Ulrich's event exactly how it was that her arm was broken in three places. They couldn't know she was wearing her only dress, nor could they understand why she was so wary of anyone trying to befriend her.

"I had not one ounce of self-esteem left," says Kathy. "I had no job skills to speak of. It was the lowest point in my life."

When Kathy slid into Ronda's pink Cadillac for a ride to an event, Ronda had no idea what a lap of luxury this car must have seemed like to this struggling woman who did her grocery shopping for a family of seven on a bicycle.

Kathy says that although she felt "lower than the dirt under the rug," the women she met through her association with Mary Kay showed her the support and praise that allowed her to begin to gather her own inner strength. It was that feeling that caused her to spend her electric bill money to purchase a showcase.

"I viewed Ronda's unit meeting as the time in my week when I could focus on something totally positive for an hour – when I could do something for *me*."

In a career filled with achievement, Ronda says, "Watching Kathy's transformation has been the most awesome 'paycheck of the heart' for me."

The most rewarding thing of all is not so much the material success she has achieved. Kathy's greatest accomplishment has been gathering her strength as a woman and a mother. "Pulling myself and my children up from the depths is something I owe to this career," Kathy says.

Karen B. Ford

The Gift of Life

She had only been a
Beauty Consultant for a year
when she got to witness firsthand
the power of a sharing culture.

Karen B. Ford and her family had rushed to be at the side of her mother after her father became critically ill.

As his condition deteriorated and after undergoing several major surgeries, the family received their share of the bill for the blood that had been required for the many transfusions. It was a staggering financial blow to her family. The hospital informed Karen's family that one way they could reduce the bill was for people to donate blood in her father's name at this particular facility.

"My Mary Kay friends had already gone overboard in helping us care for the children. Some of them volunteered to tell a few others about this situation and how they might help."

More than 170 members of the Mary Kay independent sales force – most of whom did not know Karen or her father – donated the gift of life in her father's name.

"When we got the final bill, the balance had been reduced to zero. Even the hospital personnel were amazed at the unusually high response.

"The spirit of caring and concern demonstrated by these special women just overwhelmed us. Of course, the list is kept confidential, so there was no way that I could even give a personal thank-you.

"You cannot insert this kind of caring into a how-to manual. It has to come from the very fiber of the Company. I know this caring will continue because Mary Kay has placed it at the forefront of all of our lives," says Karen.

In a career that has had many, Karen considers this the "paycheck" that meant the most.

Rena Tarbet

Committed to Keep Doing It

*She was enjoying one of those
rare days in the office
when her schedule permitted
her to take a few phone calls.*

*A*ll Rena Tarbet had a chance to say was "hello." The
woman on the other end of the phone delivered a monologue
that Rena would have had a hard time believing if she hadn't
heard it with her own ears.

The caller was an Independent Beauty Consultant who
had only dabbled at her business since marrying a surgeon
when she was 25. She went on to tell Rena that the youthful
bliss she felt when she was married hadn't lasted long before a

series of events that put the worthiness of her own life in question. Had it not been for her Mary Kay education, she said, when she found out her husband was not being faithful, and then learned her best friend had committed suicide, she would not have been able to survive.

"I freaked out and was hospitalized after I tried to overdose on prescription medicine. Once I was stabilized, they put me in the psychiatric ward where I woke up with pills, went to sleep with pills and took anti-depressants during the day. I was ready to end it all."

One day while still in the hospital, she started thinking about how great she had felt about herself when she was first starting out as a Beauty Consultant. "I had such a purpose in my life." The young woman asked a family member to bring her Mary Kay motivational tapes, including some that Rena herself had done.

She started listening to the tapes, and it wasn't long before she was released from the hospital. She told Rena, "My husband and I are going to counseling and trying to put our marriage back together. I've been working my Mary Kay business almost as a wellness therapy. I just wanted to call you and say thank you."

Rena didn't have a chance to ask or to get the woman's name or her hometown before she hung up.

"I just know that the opportunity to help someone like this is a wonderful example of how the Mary Kay way of life continues to have an enormous impact on others," Rena says. "And the most amazing thing of all is that sometimes you don't even know – you couldn't know – how you've helped. You just get a note or a call like this, truly a 'paycheck of the heart.' Then you know you must be doing something right. And you are re-committed to keep doing it."

Karen Piro

A Message to Build Our Lives On

*In 17 years she had never had a
"normal" year, and she was
hoping 1997 would be her year.*

Karen Piro stared at the two-page single-spaced letter in
disbelief. She had known Jan for 19 years. She knew some
of what had gone on in the woman's life and had at one time
organized a benefit to help raise money for some therapy
Jan needed. However, reading the letter now in its startling
totality, Karen was speechless.

With all that she had endured, Jan had taken the time to
write a letter of thanks. "Mary Kay inspires the very best in

people. This letter says it all. There is no greater 'paycheck' in the whole world," Karen says.

Jan was in the audience for Mary Kay Ash's last appearance on the Seminar stage. She had witnessed as the Company founder, whose voice was silenced by a stroke in 1996, struggled to mouth just a few words from the message that was being read in her behalf.

Miraculously, four words were audible: "You can do it."

That was all it took for Jan to pour out her own story after all these years. Jan wanted Mary Kay to know she was now certain that even through a lifetime of hardships, the career she had chosen had been a blessing. She wrote to Mary Kay:

"Your extraordinary courage, your strength, your values, your joy, your commitment to making a better world for all of us and your loving-kindness send each of us a message upon which to build our lives. You have made every year better than the last."

As Karen read the copy of the letter that had been sent to her, she was overwhelmed with how positive Jan is after all she's lived through. Her husband fought alcoholism, and she suffered a debilitating pinched nerve that confined her to her home in her first year as an Independent Sales Director. That was followed in successive years by a hysterectomy, a diagnosis of multiple sclerosis, a broken collarbone and three bouts in one year with a kidney stone. There was an aortal bypass for her husband that forced the end of his law career and breast cancer for her followed by four breast reconstructive surgeries.

In 1994, the family was celebrating its first Christmas together in the five years since their three daughters had left home. They were traveling in two cars to her father's house when the car carrying two of her daughters was hit by a drunken driver. Daughter Kerry was in a coma for three months and in and out of hospitals for the next nine months.

For 16 months following her hospital release, Kerry was in a facility being cared for by her father. She couldn't talk or move, and was able to communicate only with her thumb.

This brave Sales Director faced heart failure, blood poisoning and a collapsed lung herself before bringing her daughter to a new "handicapped accessible" home they'd built in 1997.

That same year, she wrote the letter of thanks to Mary Kay after she had earned the use of a pink car and her unit accomplished $300,000 in sales. Later in 1997, her daughter, Kerry, passed away.

Jan continues to work today, ever thankful and keenly aware that even with all the hardships she has faced, hers still manages to be a life worth living. Because of Mary Kay, Jan continues to work her business and plan the upcoming wedding of her daughter.

"What a privilege," Karen says, "to know women of strong faith like this. When people ask me what's different about Mary Kay, an example like this says it all."

Sue Kirkpatrick

Be Green and Growing

*It was yet another Mary Kay "ism" that
she passed along that day at the
self-esteem workshop she was conducting.*

"We can look at everything that happens to us in life as part of the growing process," said Sue Kirkpatrick. "We learn to save the lessons and throw the experiences away. As a result, we grow."

What Sue didn't realize as she was speaking these words was that one woman in the audience that day had hung on her every word. In fact, the woman had been close to suicide before being persuaded to come to the workshop.

The woman approached Sue afterwards, and thus began a series of personal conversations she would have with this woman to support the turnaround that began that day. "Her self-esteem was so low, I cannot even imagine how she got to that point," says Sue, whose workshop had nothing to do with her Mary Kay career. It had everything to do with Mary Kay's legacy for women.

It was that day Sue says she understood – and really realized – what it was that Mary Kay meant when she asked her sales force leaders to "pass it on."

"So many women never have an influence like Mary Kay in their lives. Mary Kay wanted not only for each of us to grow financially, but also to grow spiritually, personally and emotionally. She also wanted that for our families.

"And furthermore, she wanted us out in our communities seeing up close and personally how we could help pass along life-enriching messages to our clients, neighbors and friends."

Sue's greatest "paycheck" has been the appreciation of this gift from Mary Kay – to encourage women to be the best they can be in all areas of their lives.

"It is because of the philosophies Mary Kay instilled in me that my life mission is to pass on the personal growth I've experienced," says Sue. "Our work is never done. In fact, I believe we should always be in a growth mode."

As Mary Kay once told Sue, "We never know it all. We always need to be green and growing because when we're ripe, we wither."

Ronnie D'Esposito Klein

Of Joy and Sorrow

Many people cannot deal with talking to someone they know has a terminal illness.

Mary Kay went out of her way to make conversation that brought laughter and so much joy at a time when Steven had experienced very few of those feelings. In fact, it was in the observation of how Mary Kay Ash talked to her late husband that Ronnie D'Esposito Klcin was able to put strength in her own emotional bank account. It was a "paycheck" that paid much more than money or recognition could ever buy.

Steven was so ill that it would have been much simpler if he and Ronnie had just canceled their plans to join Mary Kay and other National Sales Directors in Canada.

From the moment they arrived, Ronnie realized it was the smartest decision she ever made.

"Mary Kay absolutely reached out to Steven and held him in a place so special. She spoke such words of comfort to him that she was able to do what no doctor or medicine or anyone had been able to do – she actually took his mind off his illness.

"He felt so loved those few days we spent in Vancouver," recalls Ronnie. "I'd like to think that Mary Kay possesses some unusual gift, but the words weren't anything out of the ordinary. It was that they came from a place so deep. It was the sense that she was speaking straight from her heart, and she was speaking so that Steven could enjoy these last precious moments." And he did.

Two weeks later Steven passed away.

Ronnie Klein will always honor the memory of that time when she experienced the greatest joy at her greatest time of sorrow.

Kathy Helou

Love Isn't Love Until You Give It Away

*Too often when bad things
happen to good people we love,
there is a feeling of
helplessness and hopelessness.*

When Kathy Helou's father left the family after a 34-year marriage, her mother was left without the skills or the will to cope with her plight. Finances made it impossible for Kathy's mom to keep the very home in which she'd raised their seven children. Pride made it impossible for her to accept help from her children – even from Kathy, who was the first Independent Sales Director to ever achieve $2 million in unit retail production.

paychecks *of the Heart*

But Kathy wasn't about to let her mom accept defeat. She had learned from Mary Kay Ash that the secret to facing obstacles is to find a way to go over, under, around and through them.

So that's what she did.

Kathy organized a "mom watch" with her siblings that lasted two years – just to make sure that her mom was OK on a daily basis. Kathy finally persuaded her mom to visit her sister in Florida and gave her mom plane tickets to get her out of town to complete her plan. No matter that Kathy knew she'd protest, they were moving mom to a new home.

While her mom was away, Kathy, her husband, Daniel, and sister-in-law, Gale, let themselves into her mom's apartment and photographed every inch of the place. They then moved all the contents to a new condominium with new furniture that they'd bought – painstakingly putting everything else back in its original place – even the photos on the fridge just the way they were.

The night her mom was to arrive home, Kathy baked her mom's favorite pie so the new place would smell like home. In a large cardboard box, she lovingly placed a full-length fur coat with her mom's name sewn in the lining and slipped one of the 34 diamond rings she's won in the pocket of the fur.

All the grandkids were gathered at the new house, per Kathy's instructions, already dressed in their pajamas for a slumber party at grandma's – "so she wouldn't have to spend the first night at the new home by herself," says Kathy.

"I've had every success any woman could ever wish for, but I have to say that seeing my mom's face that night was the greatest reward. And the amazing thing is, I couldn't help but think how proud Mary Kay would be that I have learned from her example."

Sharon Parris

Looks Can Heal

She hadn't spoken a word since arriving at the county rehabilitation home suffering from severe depression after burns left her permanently scarred.

The Palm Beach County facility thought Sharon Parris would be a great person to ask for help. Doctors there had suggested that if the woman were taught some tips on using makeup to conceal her scars, it might help her want to go on living.

Sharon was nervous, but she was more than willing to lend her expertise.

"The woman was a migrant worker who'd been carrying a vat of hot oil that spilled on her when she tripped and fell. The oil had literally burned most of her face and throat area. Most of the pigmentation had been burned away and the woman's face was a mass of huge white splotches," says Sharon.

There was some doubt among the medical personnel that she even had the will to go through another surgery she needed.

Sharon began as she had every Mary Kay skin care session – by showing the woman how to use the basic skin care products. In order to blend foundation on the scarred skin, Sharon improvised with a wash cloth. As she continued to instruct the woman on which products to use for what, the migrant worker suddenly began asking Sharon questions.

"I thought maybe I'd misunderstood what the staff had told me about her not ever speaking," says Sharon, who soon noticed nurses and doctors from throughout the center had gathered in an adjacent room to watch the transformation and, miraculously, be there to hear her speak for the first time.

As the session was ending, the woman walked over to a full-length mirror as Sharon, with tears streaming down her face, held her breath. The woman turned around to give Sharon the biggest smile, and the biggest "paycheck," she's ever received.

Jackie Swank

The Color of Success

Most people associate Mary Kay
with cosmetic products.

*T*o Jackie Swank's way of thinking, Mary Kay's success isn't about a product. It's about how the Company supports its independent sales force.

Several years ago, Jackie *watched* as an entire family's life went up in flames – all their possessions, including their home and all its contents, three cars, and the entire inventory of an up-and-coming Independent Beauty Consultant named Sandra.

Jackie's actions were at the forefront of a network of
support – Mary Kay support. It came from every place,
from the charred product order that was replaced by the
Company to the new dress purchased for Sandra by her
sister Consultants. It came from a sunshine yellow car filled
with *Mary Kay*® products that was dropped off as a loaner
from a mere acquaintance with the instructions, "use this car
as long as you need it and we'll settle up later on the
products."

Sandra, who is now an Independent Senior Sales Director,
looks back on that time with the sure knowledge that
following the fire, "Mary Kay not only became our support
system, but also it became our positive outlet to recover
from this devastation mentally, emotionally and physically."

"The message that came through to me is that Mary Kay
really cares about us and wants to see us succeed. It's not
just the product and the opportunity. It's the people."

Sandra has now earned the use of a new car to replace the
van she lost in the fire.

She found only one item in her home that wasn't charred
beyond recognition. It was a little vase in her office where

Sandra kept Company brochures. Just one portion of one brochure managed, miraculously, to go unburned or undamaged by water.

Framed today in a place of honor in her home is what remains of that brochure – a photo of Mary Kay Ash that is intact and serves as a beacon of hope that when everything went wrong in her life, onc thing went very right.

Christine Peterson

Are You From the Church, Honey?

*When your monthly check
is $65,000, sometimes
you just can't stop and
calculate what an afternoon
of your time is worth.*

She doesn't recall exactly how the woman got her name, but Christine Peterson was happy to introduce the product and the opportunity to the woman who had called. She dressed in her best suit and polished her black patent leather heels to a fine sheen. Then she packed her beauty case and drove the long distance from her home to the suburb where the woman lived.

As her sporty sedan navigated the freeways and exited onto the street, Christine knew that the neighborhood she had been called to wasn't the greatest. As she pulled up in front of the dilapidated house, Christine had to take a deep breath in order to summon the courage to go in.

A neighbor, who was out sweeping her porch, saw the perfectly coifed Christine and, as if to explain in her own mind what would bring this person to this neighborhood, the neighbor called out: "Are you from the church, honey?"

The door opened to a three-room home with two pieces of furniture – a recliner and a couch. A large ice chest served as the refrigerator.

"At first glance, I wanted to run. But as I always do when faced with a dilemma, I thought about what Mary Kay Ash would do. Clearly, I knew what she would do, and I also knew this was my chance to practice what Mary Kay has taught us," Christine recalls.

Christine didn't concern herself with what, if anything, this woman might buy. She took the opportunity to make this woman who had so little feel important. Christine allowed the woman to sample every product in her showcase.

171

When the woman's husband came home, Christine even talked the tough Marine into having a facial. Christine left some samplers for them to try. She never asked the woman about buying anything.

"I knew they had to figure out what they could afford. I sensed they were too proud to do that in front of me, so I left." Christine can't recall what the woman ordered when she called a few days later. That's not what was important. The smile on her face as she waved goodbye to Christine that day was profit enough.

This afternoon was a priceless "paycheck" in Christine's emotional bank account.

Colene Shadley

Just Fill In the Names

*Looking back over a 35-year career,
she describes the whole experience
as one big "paycheck."*

Colene Shadley has listened as several of her sister National Sales Directors are effortlessly describing their one favorite "paycheck of the heart." They all have many they could pick from, but everyone seems to be able to focus on one that was extra-special.

"I could never name just one 'paycheck' of this career. I can only say that there hasn't been one thing that wasn't in some way a 'paycheck,'" says Colene.

One particularly special moment? "They were all special."

An unbelievable time? "Too many to describe."

A story you can't forget? "Thirty-five years of them."

A memorable day?

Now there's a pause, a glint of an idea forming.

"Well," she begins slowly, "there was the day that Mary Kay Ash saved my life."

And then it pours out, with tears as profuse as the day it happened. Colene had just gone through lung cancer surgery with her mother.

Colene discovered a lump in her breast.

"I was so afraid. I didn't dare tell my husband. I didn't dare tell anybody. I decided to just pretend it wasn't there."

Not long after, Colene was in Dallas and she told Mary Kay. "Mary Kay left the meeting and placed an immediate call to her own doctor," says Colene.

It was a Tuesday.

Wednesday, Colene was sent to the hospital for tests.

Thursday, she had surgery.

She also returned to Dallas to take her chemotherapy. "Without Mary Kay I don't think I could have made it." Mary Kay knew instinctively how to help Colene battle the doubts and depression every cancer patient faces.

Each time Colene arrived, her sister NSD, Idell Moffett, would pick her up and take her by Mary Kay's new house which was in the process of being built. "Mary Kay would sometimes pretend that she couldn't decide on something so that I could help her pick a color or a style. She tried to help me keep my mind off my illness."

One particularly low day as she was departing Dallas, Colene received an envelope from Mary Kay's assistant. Inside there was a note: "Mary Kay thought it might help your Sales Directors to hear from you, so we put together this little newsletter."

"That was the day I knew I could fight this battle and win." says Colene, who has been cancer-free for 14 years.

Doris Jannke

The Meaning of Go-Give

She was anxious to board her flight
so she could get in a good nap.

oris Jannke secured her seatbelt, closed her eyes and was just about to drift off when she overheard something said by the lady seated next to her. She opened her eyes for just an instant, and in that second, she was recognized.

The woman nudged her husband and whispered loud enough for anyone to hear. "She's a National Sales Director. Maybe we could ask her!"

There goes the nap, Doris thought at the same time that Mary Kay's sweet voice echoed in her sleepy head. "If we help enough people get what they want, our lives will be richly blessed."

This is the main premise of something that Mary Kay Ash calls "go-give," the unselfish act of reaching out to help when there is nothing in it for you. Tired as she was, Doris knew she had to take the time to help these strangers.

Doris turned her attention to answering all the couple's questions. It was their first Seminar, and they were anxious to take the lessons they'd learned and build a strong business. "I want a car. I want to be a Sales Director," said the woman.

During the entire three-and-a-half-hour flight, they talked and planned. Doris shared all the wisdom she had with the eager couple. She handed them her card as she left the airport.

A bouquet of daisies for Doris arrived the next day from the couple.

Six months later, she heard that the woman on the airplane had earned the use of a car and had become a Sales Director.

As chance would have it, a few months later one of Doris'
new team members was moving to the town where this
newfound friend lived. Doris called her, and when the new
team member relocated, she was "adopted" by this Sales
Director and her unit.

"They welcomed her like family," says Doris.

Ree Foster

Bonds to Treasure

*The relationships that develop between
a Mary Kay Beauty Consultant and
her customers are special indeed.*

As Ree Foster was checking her messages late one afternoon, she was shocked by a message she received from a nurse at the local hospital.

"There is a patient who's just desperate to see you," the caller said.

Ree returned the call and was told that the nurse had been told to call about makeup.

It turned out that one of her customers was hospitalized and so sick that her husband had been called stateside from overseas military duty. When she learned he was on the plane bound for home, the patient panicked.

"Just please," she told Ree, "make me look pretty for my husband."

Ree grabbed her beauty case and rushed to the woman's side. By the time her husband arrived, the woman was looking and feeling a lot better. Ree cried all the way home.

"It has always touched me deeply that in her desperation she thought of calling me.

"When she thought she was going to die and wanted to look good for her husband, she thought of her Mary Kay Beauty Consultant. That's a very special relationship. It's a bond that so many of us have come to treasure."

The patient survived. She's still one of Ree's customers today.

Linda Kirkbride

A Commitment to Care

It was the first time she had been at a hospital since her mom died in a hospital room.

Linda Kirkbride had gotten a call from one of her unit members who had sold a nail care set from her hospital bed and asked if Linda would bring it to the hospital.

"It didn't hit me until I walked down the hall. 'Oh, Linda, come on, be a big girl. Don't get shook up about this. But I couldn't do it.'" Linda decided to find a nurse and let her give the gravely ill patient the products. "I couldn't go in that room. I just felt like I was going to totally break down."

Memories of her mother's death and knowing the Beauty
Consultant was dying overwhelmed Linda.

The nurse grabbed Linda's arm and said, "Oh, no. You have to
go in and see her. She's told us all about you."

The patient, Peggy, was thrilled to see her special visitor.
Linda managed to maintain her composure while they
visited. Just as she was leaving, Peggy said, "You know, Linda,
Mary Kay is going to want to know that I'm in the hospital."

Linda cried all the way home. Peggy really believed that the
chairman of this Company was going to call her. She didn't
know exactly how, but she was determined that someone at
Mary Kay headquarters would at least send a card. Through
her tears she left a message on the Company "care hot line"
with the hospital address.

The next morning Linda's phone rang. It was Mary Kay's
assistant calling to find out what was wrong with Peggy and
how could Mary Kay reach her. Linda sobbed as she gave out
the number. She cried out of sheer joy that Mary Kay herself
would take the time to place such a call. She cried because
she had forgotten for a moment that this wasn't just any
corporation. This is Mary Kay.

Peggy, weak but happy, called Linda the next day so excited about the phone call. "Mary Kay and I chatted like old girlfriends, and we talked about having things tucked and taken out," Peggy said.

Linda cried tears of joy.

"I'm ready to go now, Linda."

One final sale and a phone call from Mary Kay. It was all Peggy needed.

Anita Mallory Garrett-Roe

Take the Roses With the Thorns

*She was one of the pioneers
who helped put Mary Kay on
the map in Minnesota, so
Mary Kay Ash decided to visit.*

Someone thought it would be wonderful if every sales force member who brought a new team member to the special event would have the honor of walking onstage to present Mary Kay with a beautiful long-stemmed pink rose.

The Mary Kay appearance was held in a huge arena, and just as they had planned, a long line of sales force members went onstage and each handed Mary Kay a rose. Mary Kay graciously held the bouquet even though it got bigger and heavier by the minute. She smiled throughout.

When the presentation was finally over, Anita and several other hosts of the event removed the roses "from her precious little arms." What they saw horrified them. There were punctures and droplets of blood on Mary Kay's arms – many of the roses had not been de-thorned. "Oh, Mary Kay, you're bleeding!" was all that Anita could muster the courage to say.

True to Mary Kay's strength of spirit, she was not about to let anyone know this had happened, and she certainly wasn't going to let it ruin this special evening for anyone.

Without uttering a word, she shook her head and went right on with the program – including making a spirited speech delivered with enthusiasm.

Anita saw that day how Mary Kay lived the lessons she taught, and she considers it one of the many "paychecks" of her career that she learned these lessons firsthand. Anita adds, "Mary Kay always taught us to overcome whatever difficulties we must face, to always keep a positive attitude and not tell your problems. This memory has always served as an example of Mary Kay living her philosophy."

Valerie Bagnol

Eat Your Dessert!

When she's nervous, she doesn't eat.
She never thought anyone would notice.

It was her first Mary Kay trip and Valerie Bagnol was excited about qualifying to travel to Switzerland with the other top Sales Directors. At the first formal dinner on the trip, Valerie had absolutely no appetite.

"I was watching all these wonderfully talented women and feeling so excited to be in the company of them. I was thrilled that Mary Kay herself joined us for dinner," recalls Valerie, but, of course, "I couldn't eat. I just picked at each course."

In order to visit with everyone, Mary Kay moved to a different table for each course of the banquet. Mary Kay joined her table for dessert.

"Then, I *really* couldn't eat!"

"Valerie, eat your dessert. I've noticed you've barely touched your food all evening. With your figure you can certainly afford to eat dessert!" said Mary Kay.

At that moment, Valerie felt like a small child being tenderly watched over by a loved one looking out for her well being. "Wow. I couldn't believe she noticed and cared whether I ate or not!"

"The one thing about Mary Kay that has always impressed me," says Valerie, "is that she doesn't just give lip service to treating people kindly. She treats everyone as she would want to be treated. It's funny, but that night I felt so loved and so special. I can't remember feeling that way since I was a young child and my grandmother would fuss over me."

Family Matters

"Learn to evaluate

your success

by the balance

you achieve

in your life."

Sandy Miller

What Eddie Had Become

*Sandy Miller was watching
the press conference when
Michael Jordan announced his
retirement from basketball.
She burst into tears.*

She wasn't crying because Jordan was leaving basketball. It's just that Sandy had caught sight of her son, Eddie, who was working the event as an ESPN sports radio intern.

It wasn't seeing Eddie that caused her to cry, it was seeing the Eddie he had become.

Sandy emotionally recalls the heart-to-heart conversation she'd had with Mary Kay some 22 years before. It was that conversation which Sandy believes led her son to this wonderful day when he was accomplishing all the goals he had yearned for. And while the rest of a national television audience was watching the basketball hero, Sandy was looking at her son as a hero.

Years before, Sandy had confided in Mary Kay how worried she was about Eddie's health. He was only three years old when Sandy learned he had serious learning differences. Mary Kay comforted Sandy, reminding her how it is possible for the human spirit to overcome what might seem like daunting obstacles.

Mary Kay told Sandy, "If you have the choice of giving your son a million dollars or giving him a positive attitude, choose the attitude."

Sandy recalls, "Mary Kay looked me straight in the eye and she said 'it will be worth so much more than millions.'"

Five days after Sandy returned home from her Dallas trip, there came a handwritten card in the mail to Eddie. "To a three-year-old! Now, he couldn't comprehend what it meant for a CEO to be writing him, but I could," says Sandy. "That card and our conversation strengthened my resolve. That day, I knew Eddie would be okay and, at that moment, my own belief in this Company strengthened. I knew then I'd be a Mary Kay lifer!"

As Eddie grew up to graduate from Purdue University and pursue his sports broadcasting passion, Sandy hung on to that now-tattered card.

"For me it represented that Eddie was going to be OK. I think seeing him on TV that day just cemented what I'd been feeling in my heart all those years."

Anne Newbury

The Prize

*"It felt like I was the one
awarding the lottery."*

*A*s a consistent Top 10 Independent National Sales
Director, Anne Newbury had already traveled to all the major
ports of the world with her husband, Lane, courtesy of
Mary Kay. By the time the 1988 contest prizes were
announced, Anne had become accustomed to her mother's
sweet refrain each time she was packing: "I wish you could
pack me in the baggage compartment!"

Anne learned there was a new twist to those earning the
top tier trip that year. You could take anyone you wanted for
10 glorious days of first-class travel complete with private

car and driver in Italy. At her husband's suggestion, Anne and her area got busy and earned the trip as a gift for her mother. She added some of her and Lane's favorite European cities to the itinerary and she extended the length of stay. Then Anne told her mother to start packing!

"It felt like I was the one awarding the lottery," says Anne, who describes her mother as being like a kid in a candy store through the entire trip. "We had a ball!"

Nothing in Anne's life could compare to the feelings she had during that time when she was able not only to make her mother's dreams come true but also to share such a special time.

Anne's mother, who had never been ill a day in her life, died unexpectedly two years later.

"I remember Mary Kay telling us we should never put off until tomorrow the things that we need to do today. Out of that experience, I have the fondest memories and the most priceless 'paycheck' of all."

Sharon Kingrey

Not Just A Ribbon

*There is great value in making
people feel important.*

Mary Kay Ash has said that if she were to teach a course in management, she would require all the students to wear a "make me feel important" sign for the entire semester. "By the end of the term and for the rest of their lives, they'd imagine seeing the same sign hanging from the neck of everyone they meet."

Sharon Kingrey has heard this Mary Kay message countless times during her career: People crave recognition. People like to feel important.

There was one example right under her nose, but Sharon says she didn't even realize it until recently when she found a ribbon among her son's most valued awards.

Mary Kay Ash once gave her young son, John, a ribbon that said, "You Are Special." Sharon thought it was a nice gesture, just like the personal letters all three of her children received from Mary Kay through the years. They were great conversation pieces. Adults would always marvel that a CEO wrote to children. And certainly, these were items to be stored away in a scrapbook.

But Sharon had no idea how important this ribbon was to her son.

Although he is in college taking premed courses now, the ribbon he received from Mary Kay holds a special place in John's heart. Perhaps, his mom says, it was John's first taste of feeling important, his first sense of achievement. Mary Kay thought he was special – and she made him feel important. It was a feeling John never forgot.

John treasures that ribbon today – as much as his Eagle Scout medal and the Most Outstanding Senior award his teachers gave him in high school. The Mary Kay ribbon holds a place of honor alongside his valedictorian certificate, the National Honor Society pin and his captain's medal from the regional basketball championship season.

"The way my son feels about that little, inexpensive ribbon is a symbol to me of how easy it is to motivate people to greatness. In my mind, it represents how very important praise can be," says Sharon.

Wynne Lou Ferguson

The One Constant In My Life

One moment in time that
was melancholy, sweet,
heartbreaking, loving.

Wynne Lou Ferguson's husband, Clyde, was in a Dallas hospital being treated for cancer during Seminar 1994. Mary Kay invited them both to her hotel suite for a visit. With special permission from his physician and the assistance of his nurses in the hospital, Clyde was able to make the visit.

"The nurses dressed him in his suit," Wynne Lou recalls, "and put him in a cab to join me at the hotel.

"Clyde was a great big rancher, six-four and gregarious, with a very commanding presence," says Wynne Lou. "When we arrived, he sat with Mary Kay on a small settee and she held his hands in hers. She stroked his cheek. I witnessed one of those moments in time that was melancholy, sweet, heartbreaking and loving all at the same time.

"Mary Kay was saying her 'goodbye.' Both of them knew what I was about to face. I think in her own way, Mary Kay was letting Clyde know that I would be OK."

When Clyde died a few weeks later, Mary Kay was one of the first to arrive at the hospital to give comfort and sympathy. It was only later that Wynne Lou learned that this same hospital room was the one where Mary Kay's beloved husband, Mel, had died just a few years before.

Today, Wynne Lou shares her story in the hopes that her experience will help other women.

"I never share my story with women without telling them how – without this career – I would have been terrified at finding myself widowed at the age of 48 with three children in college. I had a large debt on our cattle and ranch land.

Because I had achieved National Sales Director status the previous year, I was prepared to financially take care of my children and myself."

Wynne Lou feels she was also emotionally bolstered. "I learned during this painful time that aside from my faith and my family, Mary Kay was the one constant in my life."

Diane Underwood

Lessons Caught, Not Taught

*The ability to instill in her own
daughters the gifts that
her career instilled in her has
been the greatest reward.*

At the outset of her Mary Kay career, Diane Underwood instantly liked the positive attitude she found in all the women she met.

Even though her daughters have grown up in the Mary Kay world, Diane still manages to be amazed at all the subtle lessons they've learned from their mom and her friends. Now that they're grown, seeing what they've learned manifest itself in their lives has become Diane's greatest "paycheck."

"Working this career allowed me all the wonderful benefits of a flexible schedule. I was able to attend their track meets and accompany them when their band marched in the Orange Bowl parade.

"I was home in the afternoons when they came home from school and needed to talk about their day. I was by their side when they were sick and right there when the phone call came for their first date."

Those, Diane concedes, are the obvious benefits. She recalls once hearing Mary Kay speak on the fact that what is *caught* by children is often more significant than what is *taught*. Diane wasn't sure what that meant until recently when she observed the manner in which her daughters treat people and in the way they react to challenges.

"They were noticing even when I wasn't trying to set an example."

They noticed the small things, like how their mom took time to compliment a stranger on what she was wearing. And they noticed bigger ones, like how their mom motivated herself even when the work seemed overwhelming.

I would always say, "If I'm going to make my goals this year, then I have to work even when I don't feel like it."

One recent night when her daughter, Nikki, came to ask if Diane would go out for a run with her (she's not allowed to run alone at night), Diane said she was too tired and didn't feel like it.

Nikki, sounding very much like her mother, replied, "I'm too tired, too, but if I'm going to be good in track this year, I need to run even when I don't feel like it." The message registered. Off they went for the run.

"Mary Kay is so right. The lessons caught – not just those that are taught – are the ones from which they learn the most," says Diane.

Joanne Holman

Of Hamsters and Humans

The note was only two sentences long,
but it conveyed everything
you'd ever want to know about
Mary Kay's humanity.

Joanne Holman had won the honor of having Mary Kay visit an event she hosted in her home state. Eleven hundred people attended the event and it went off very smoothly. Joanne had no sooner heaved a great sigh of relief than she had to come up with a plan for what to do with the living legend in her midst before it was time to take her to the airport.

They decided to pass the extra time at Joanne's home.

"Three steps into my front door, Mary Kay had kicked off her shoes and transformed herself from famous dignitary to family friend stopping by for a visit."

The Holman's 8-year-old daughter, Jeri, was spellbound by the thought that this woman she'd heard her mom talk about was now in her house. She ran upstairs to retrieve her prized possession, and before Joanne could intervene, Jeri was handing her hamster to Mary Kay. Joanne was horror-struck until she watched this woman who'd just wowed more than a thousand women cradle that furry little bundle named Misty in her arms and lovingly pet it.

A few days after the visit, Mary Kay sent a personal note to Jeri. In two sentences, Mary Kay illustrated for Joanne the greatest example of how the smallest kindness can have the biggest impact.

> *Dear Jeri:*
> *I very much enjoyed meeting your hamster, Misty. I know you must be very proud of your mom, as we here at the Company are.*

"In two sentences, Mary Kay had," as Joanne says,
"• Shown an eight-year-old that she counted, too;

- Shown a little girl that Mary Kay cared about what was important to her by remembering the name of the hamster;
- Let Jeri know her mom was special by praising me;
- Made me feel special by praising me to my daughter; and
- Demonstrated that no one should be too busy, or too famous, to be kind and thoughtful.

"As great as her accomplishments are in commerce, it is Mary Kay, the person, who inspires in me the greatest pride in the human race," Joanne says.

You're a Winner !
Carol Anton
SNSD

Carol Anton

Family Business

*Anytime there's a family gathering
at the Anton's, there are at least three
pink Cadillacs in the driveway.*

Mary Kay is a family business in Carol Anton's family.

In 1974, when she became an Independent Beauty Consultant right out of college, Carol – who had married and moved – only knew three people she might share her business with: her new mother-in-law and one friend each of her two sisters-in-law.

She had no idea then that, in due time, her two sisters-in-law and her mother-in-law would find the same excitement and success that she had found in Mary Kay.

"I've often teased my husband that the reason the Lord sent him is because there was so much untapped talent in his family! They needed a vehicle. Mary Kay was the vehicle and I was the messenger," says Carol.

There is, says Carol, a whole new complexity and much joy from being bonded in this special way in your business. The women have a special closeness shared by best friends. The four family members share business expertise, ideas and the joy of each other's successes.

Carol recently heard of one family with four generations of women who are part of the independent sales force. "What a beautiful and remarkable testament to the Company that women of four generations would find a commonality and a calling to the same career!

"That's how it is with us! It's a 'paycheck of the heart' to see your family prosper and flourish with this opportunity. To see them be able to design their lives with God as the first priority; family values and ethics second; and love, compassion and integrity in business as the third priority warms my heart," says Carol.

"I shudder to think where their lives would be without Mary Kay. This career fits each of them like a glove. You simply cannot put a price tag on the sense of true blessing that comes from being the one that opened the door of opportunity for your own family!"

Sheron Flaster

What the Mind Can Believe

When her son received his doctorate,
Sheron Flaster had a flashback
to a chance meeting that
probably got him started on
his academic course.

She had taken her two young sons on the trip to Washington, D.C., because of the educational possibilities. Sheron Flaster had no idea what an education her son would get. From Mary Kay Ash.

Royce, then 10, rode with Mary Kay Ash in the hotel elevator one day. She struck up a conversation and asked the young boy what his goals were. He explained that he was interested in printing and publishing. She had arrived at her floor by then, so Mary Kay suggested they meet for a personal conference the next day to discuss his business and his goals. She told Royce to meet her at the side of the stage.

"Royce burst into our hotel room that day full of confidence and feeling so important," Sheron recalls. Royce did meet with Mary Kay and she later wrote to encourage him to pursue his goals.

And he did, according to Sheron. "He never forgot that experience and how Mary Kay looked him right in the eye. How she paid attention to him. How she made him feel important." Royce received his Ph.D. in English and is currently an English professor. Sheron remembers Mary Kay teaching her that the mind is the place where all progress begins and ends. "She has always told us that if your mind can conceive it, and if you can believe it, you can achieve it."

Pat Fortenberry

"I'm Not Great Today, But I'm Working On It."

To see the vivacious blonde, one would imagine that she'd never had a care in the world.

*P*at Fortenberry has been a consistent top performer in her Mary Kay career, and even had the joy of watching her own daughter, Pam, achieve some of the great rewards of this career. The greatest reward both say they've achieved, however, has nothing to do with beauty, money or fame.

It has to do with attitude. And their attitude has been a blessing.

When Pam's young son, Jacob, was born, the celebration was cut short by the news that he had cystic fibrosis (CF). When

Mary Kay called to see how they were doing, Pat recalls that her daughter gave a different twist to the expected answer Mary Kay was accustomed to hearing.

It is part of the Mary Kay legend that whenever she asks you how you're doing, the answer should be nothing less than "great." Mary Kay has been known to ask a person the question again and again until they give her the answer she wants to hear.

This day, however, Mary Kay knew what was behind Pam's answer. She understood what Pam meant when she said, "I'm not great today, but I'm working on it."

Before they finished talking, Pam had assured Mary Kay that, "Jacob's going to be fine, and we will be, too." And then Pam, her husband, Alex, and the grandparents went about making that so.

Jacob has reached the age of 6 without ever having been hospitalized – a rarity for CF sufferers.

With a one in four chance of having a second child born with CF, Pam's second child, Katie, also has the congenital disease.

Pat believes that her daughter's Mary Kay upbringing is the reason she's been able to cope with these challenges so competently. "As she told me one day shortly after Katie was born, 'Mom, the Lord knew who to give these children to. We have the positive outlook and the can-do attitude that it takes.'"

Pat has turned her energies to helping raise funds for cystic fibrosis research.

Julie Krebsbach

If It Is To Be, It's Up To Me

This Iowa farm girl had to really work up the nerve to attend her first Mary Kay function in Chicago.

$\mathcal{L}$uckily, her children have come to understand at a very young age the rewards of goal setting and achieving your dreams. "Already they understand better than I did that there is a great big world out there for exploring," said Julie Krebsbach, whose blended family includes two daughters and one son.

It was through her stepdaughter's eyes that Julie received the finest "paycheck" of her career. It was the autobiographical essay for advanced placement English class written by Tonia following her attendance at the 1995 Mary Kay Seminar in which Julie made her debut as a National Sales Director.

Tonia wrote that her first clue that she was a VIP was when she and her sister attended one of the many pre-Seminar parties their mom had been invited to. The girls had stepped out of the hotel ballroom without taking their identification badges and upon their return they were stopped.

"I calmly explained that we are the daughters of Julie Krebsbach, and the woman quickly apologized for not recognizing us, then let us back in. I felt like a movie star – someone so important that the door woman was afraid that she had offended me," Tonia wrote.

She talked about sitting four rows from the massive Dallas Convention Center stage. "I could feel the intensity of the lights on my face; I could hear the heavy breathing of the dancers."

She wished out loud that she could actually meet Mary Kay, and her dad was able to make this wish come true. Her words:

> *"About halfway through the ceremony, my dad*
> *came rushing over to my sister and me and*
> *ordered us to go with him. We thought something*

awful had happened. My heart began to pound; terrible thoughts went through my head. Maybe my stepmother had fallen and broken a bone; maybe she had fainted or become ill. My father led us to a small room surrounded by men in suits. My mind was racing with what I would find on the other side of that door. When the door opened, I felt my heart race faster and I began to tremble. I was in Mary Kay's private, backstage room. Mary Kay took my hand and kissed my cheek. She continued to hold my hand, and I was thinking about how short she actually was and how soft her hands were."

The paper's conclusion:

"I never thought that one person could make such a difference in someone's life. With her opportunities and her genuine sincerity, Mary Kay has changed so many women's lives. I learned a great deal on my trip to Texas, but the most important lesson from Seminar for me is that I need to set goals for myself and I must put forth the effort to attain my goals. If I do so, then I will also be rewarded. Perhaps not on a glamorous stage, but in my own heart and mind."

Janis Moon

The Trip Not Missed

*She was pursuing an advanced
degree in nursing, so she
expected to spend lots of time
in a hospital environment.*

Janis Moon never expected that she'd be moving into a hospital to nurse her 9-month-old baby back to health. She really never expected she'd be running her Mary Kay business from that hospital room for two months.

"Whenever I am relating the benefits of this career, I always recall this example. Because it happened to me so early in motherhood, this made me realize that I would never have been able to care for my son and continue earning an income from any other kind of career.

"I never would have been able to put my son first. Being your own boss means not having to ask permission for time off," says Janis.

Janis knows that one of the greatest obstacles facing working mothers is finding the time to be there for their kids in times of great need – like an illness. She also knows that "because I had the choices I did, I'll never regret not being there for my kids." She thanks her stars every day she started her business right out of college.

This is a message Janis wants all mothers to hear, along with the message she once got from Mary Kay.

Janis had qualified for and then had to miss a top Sales Director trip because her son was in the hospital. Janis talked to Mary Kay about being pulled between family obligations and career perks. Mary Kay's words were the best "paycheck" she ever got.

"Mary Kay told me that it wasn't actually taking the trip that was important. It was knowing I'd earned it. And then she assured me there would be plenty of time left for trips when the boys were a little older."

When Janis qualified for and wasn't able to attend at least two additional trips due to her son's birth, Mary Kay's words stayed with her.

By the time she became one of the youngest Independent National Sales Directors in the nation, Janis realized that she and her husband would have the next 20 years to make up for any trips she may have missed.

Debi R. Moore

In Good Times and In Bad

*To Debi Moore's way of thinking,
a career is a lot like a marriage.
It should be there as a support
in good times and in bad.*

*D*ebi had dabbled at her business as a Beauty Consultant, not knowing whether or not this was the right career move for her. She kept thinking she belonged in a corporate environment - or at least in a classroom teaching. She kept searching for clues.

Her Mary Kay business was unfolding beautifully, and Debi had just given birth to her first child when she got the answer.

221

"My mom had flown out to visit us and see her new grandchild. The day before she was to leave, she collapsed," Debi recalls. The diagnosis was an inoperable brain tumor.

Within 48 hours of this tragic news, Debi had a personal phone call from Mary Kay, who spent more than an hour on the phone with the fledgling Independent Sales Director. During the call, Debi expressed the frustration of not knowing what to do about her business while she attended to her mom. She needed the income. She feared it wouldn't be there for her if she cut back on her work.

Debi will never forget Mary Kay's words. Years later they bring tears.

"Debi, this Company will always be here. You need to take the time off to spend with your mother now."

So Debi took the time to travel three states away with her baby in tow to be with her mom. Throughout the ordeal, her customers continued calling and her team members continued working. And her career choice provided the emotional support she needed so badly to sustain her the year her mother passed away. It was during that year that she made up her mind to go all the way to the top in this, her chosen profession.

"You can work at anything to make money, but you will never have the emotional support when the bottom falls out of your life like I did with Mary Kay. Although it was a very painful time in my life, I learned that this was the difference.

"I learned that my company would be there for me in the good times and the bad."

Ann Robinette

Sons Speak Louder Than Words

She liked to think that she had been able to put her family before her career, to keep her priorities in order while building a successful business.

At least that's what she thought she had done. Ann Robinette wasn't to find out until years later her sons' opinions.

Her son, Gary, in his late 30s, received quite an unusual phone call one afternoon. The woman was calling to ask if he was Ann Robinette's son. He assured her he was Ann's son, and then she told him the reason for her call.

"I have four teenagers. I've heard your mother say many times that she put her family first, and I was wondering if you'd agree that she did. I'm just not sure it's possible in any career to do that."

Gary thought for a moment and then he said, "Well, ma'am, to tell you the truth, my brother and I never realized that our mom worked. For years we would volunteer her to do all kinds of things at school and sports that the other mothers wouldn't be able to do. When we grew up, it came as a complete surprise to us that our mom was one of the most successful women in Mary Kay."

The words – repeated to Ann by her son – made Ann's heart sing.

Interestingly, Gary's brother, Patrick, also picked up this same theme when he was asked to speak at his mother's National Sales Director debut. Patrick took the microphone and he spoke words that were music to his mother's heart.

"Ladies, if you build your business on the axiom of Mary Kay priorities – God first, family second, career third – you will be successful. I never remember my mother not having a hot breakfast for us on a cold winter morning. And I never remember her missing a ballgame."

Ann smiles as she recalls her sons' words. "My goal was to never have to look back and wish I had done something different. I achieved it!"

Irmel Boyle-Schulz

The Opportunity of the Land

*If the line hadn't been so long that day
at the printer where she had her
newsletter duplicated, she would have
driven right onto the accident scene to see
four of her five children injured.*

Irmel Boyle-Schulz had waved at her kids when she passed them on the road to the printer. It was only moments later the accident happened.

The most seriously injured was her daughter, Beatrice, then 18. Her injuries required that she be in a body cast for an entire year.

Irmel's family had only recently moved to California from Hawaii, and she was just beginning to rebuild her Mary Kay business there after having been the first Sales Director in Hawaii.

Now it would be necessary to take a year off to care for Beatrice.

"She was literally locked in a prison for a year. We never traveled and we never went anywhere. I had to do everything for her," Irmel recalls.

Even though this happened in 1978, Irmel says that was when she realized what a wonderful career she had stumbled onto. Even in a year of rebuilding in a new state when she had to care full time for her injured daughter, Irmel earned $12,000 more that year than the year before!

"The uniqueness of this opportunity can really be summed up in that one fact. It is exactly as Mary Kay explained it to me. You spend a few years paying your dues, and then you spend so much time enjoying the fruits of your labor."

Having grown up in postwar Germany, Irmel was extremely appreciative of the opportunities that could be found in

America. She had often heard the expression that "America is the land of opportunity."

Irmel would agree. And she would add: Mary Kay is the opportunity of the land.

Nan Stroud

Never, Never, Never

It was 24 Decembers ago,
but for Nan Stroud the words
ring loud and clear – as loud
and clear as the heavenly
notes she just heard her daughter
sing in a Christmas concert.

"Mary Kay gave me the confidence to dig and hunt and ask and call. That day, she gave me permission not to be intimidated by the news I'd received."

Mary Kay gave Nan belief in her daughter's future again on that dark and cold December day.

The young mother had just learned that her oldest child was learning challenged and couldn't continue in the classes she needed in the local school system. In 1975, kids like hers, more often than not, fell through the cracks and often were institutionalized.

"I called Mary Kay because I didn't have anyone else I thought would understand," says Nan. "Mary Kay told me to keep looking for options. Never, never, never give up."

She told Nan, "You must accept the worst. Then put every bit of energy into working constantly for what's best for your daughter."

That piece of advice was all Nan needed. She hung up the phone with renewed hope and enough confidence to move mountains. The assertiveness Nan had learned as a result of her Mary Kay career helped immensely as she set out to gather experts from across the state to help her appeal for appropriate education for her daughter and others in the same situation.

Nan's work paid off. Counselors began paying attention to the special needs kids in her state, and training began in new techniques for working with the learning challenged.

"As I worked, I stayed focused by recalling Mary Kay's message. The message, 'Put every bit of your energy into working for what's best,' became the greatest 'paycheck' of my heart."

Nan's daughter completed high school. Today she lives a wonderful and full young life. She's married, works and has a beautiful home. She also sings in the church choir.

"Every time I look at her," Nan says, "I see the miracle that came as a result of Mary Kay sharing her belief and giving me the strength to do what needed to be done."

Linda Cole-McBroom

The Moment of Silence

It is the phone call that
every mother dreads.

The predominantly female audiences at Mary Kay Seminars
are always cordial to handsome gentlemen who appear
onstage. Chris got that same kind of recognition as he
escorted his mother Linda Cole-McBroom onto the stage
for her National Sales Director debut.

Chris blushed, but then his demeanor turned very serious.
He took the microphone.

He paused, took several deep breaths and began to speak.
"I came today to thank you for the prayers. I went into

surgery at 10 a.m. two summers ago. I was still in the operating room as your Awards Night began. Mary Kay Ash opened the evening with a silent moment of prayer in my behalf.

"I believe each one of you is responsible for my survival and my recovery, and I came to thank you."

The strapping young man handed Mary Kay a bouquet of flowers as tears streamed down his face. He continued,

"The nurses and doctors thought I must be somebody famous. I told them I'm not a celebrity, but I am a member of the Mary Kay family," Chris said to booming applause.

Linda had been in Dallas celebrating her first-time status as a million-dollar Sales Director when she received a phone call that her son, Chris, had been hospitalized.

It is the phone call that every mother dreads.

She rushed home to find he'd already been scheduled for brain surgery.

The first person Linda called was Pat Fortenberry, her Senior National Sales Director. She was on the next plane and slept alongside Linda at the hospital throughout Chris' life-threatening ordeal. The entire Mary Kay world kept Chris in constant prayer.

Linda is certain of one thing. She would give back every prize, every bit of recognition and her entire commission earnings. "The only things I would insist on keeping are the rewards and benefits that money cannot buy. No amount of money could ever replace the support network, the closeness of true friends of my heart, and the strength it gave to my son and our entire family during this trying time."

Ruell Cone

You're My Hero

She eagerly opened the letter
from her daughter, never
knowing that inside was
the finest compliment
she could ever be paid.

Even when the contents of her entire home consisted of two trundle beds, a refrigerator and a piano, Ruell Cone knew that the seeds of greatness were within her.

After her first four skin care classes, Ruell had lots of reason to quit. She spilled everything onto the floor at the first class, got lost going to the second, found no one at home for her third and forgot one of the five steps in the regimen at the fourth class.

But Ruell persisted. And all the while her three children were watching. They listened as she worked with pride, determination, perseverance and courage.

She used her Mary Kay teachings to inspire her children. And she used all her earnings to make sure they had every opportunity. As the daughter of sharecroppers, Ruell was motivated by a burning desire to help them make their dreams come true.

When Mary Kay heard what Ruell was doing with her earnings, she told Ruell "that's the wisest investment you could ever make." With earnings from her Mary Kay career, Ruell put three children through college and medical school, and because they were all born within three years of each other, the triple tuition came all at once.

Today, Cecil is a pathologist, Charleston is an internist, and Anita specializes in sports medicine.

One year after Anita had attended Stanford University, and then studied French in Paris before going on to Howard University, she wrote her mother a letter. For the price of a stamp – and a daughter's unbridled gratitude – it is the finest "paycheck" Ruell has ever received. Anita wrote:

"I have met so many wonderful, talented and famous people in all of my travels and in my studies. But I have to say, mom, you are the most famous of them all."

Nydia Payán

Destinies So Different

*When she thinks about her mother's
life, she is amazed at the
life-changing differences that can
happen in just one generation.*

From earliest childhood, Nydia Payán remembers that
America was the land her mother always admired. She
yearned for her daughters to live in the land of opportunity
even though she really had no idea what opportunity for a
woman really was. Her mother's dreams would eventually
become reality when she emigrated from Nicaragua,
followed shortly thereafter by her five daughters.

"My mother died in the country she loved surrounded by the love of her children. I only wish she could have lived to see my dreams come true. They were such different dreams than my mother's," says Nydia.

Nydia's dream was to be successful in business. She wanted to be a professional who could enjoy the talents with which God had blessed her.

"Mary Kay gave me the means to accomplish what I wanted. I would have the opportunity to change people's lives for the better! I would be able to educate my children at accomplished universities and travel around the world with my husband!"

"For me and so many others, Mary Kay is an angel sent from heaven to help make dreams a reality."

These were dreams Nydia knows her own mother could not even imagine.

Family Matters

Business
Sensitivity

"As we journey

through life,

the most valuable

assets we carry with us

are our integrity,

our reputation and

the good, honest name

upon which we can

build our future."

Joan Rector

Keep Hope Alive

She was a terrific, hardworking
housekeeper who had everything
she needed to make a go
of a Mary Kay career. It took
her 20 years to get there.

Goodness knows, Joan Rector thought, this woman needed everything this career had to offer. She was willing to pay for her showcase by working off the cost in housekeeping services. It took her three months to finally afford to make that purchase.

"The day her showcase arrived she broke down and cried, thanking me for opening this great door of opportunity for her," Joan recalls.

"The trouble was, every time she'd get a few dollars ahead, her son would get into trouble again and she'd be back in debt. The poor woman could never get ahead."

Joan tried to help the woman, but eventually Joan moved, they lost touch and the woman let go of her Mary Kay business.

Last year, Joan was speaking at a guest event in the city where she formerly lived. A woman came up and introduced herself, never imagining Joan would remember her. Joan did and greeted her with a big hug.

"It took me almost 20 years to get my troubles under control, but during all that time, not a day went by that I didn't think about the Mary Kay opportunity," the woman said.

"I am about to earn the use of my first car, and I'm determined not to stop until I'm driving a pink car!

"Thank you, Joan, for the dream that kept me alive and now is coming true."

Stacy James

Do the Right Thing

*The records won't reflect
that she got a new
team member that day.*

She was well on her way to achieving the pinnacle of a Mary Kay career. In wrapping up her goal to become a National Sales Director, Stacy James only needed to add a few team members to realize success.

She had interviewed hundreds of women during her Mary Kay career. Some she never heard from again. Some became part of her team. But as she interviewed this woman and her husband, Stacy was preoccupied by what seemed like a troubled situation in the marriage.

She grappled with what she sensed, and while one part of her wanted to reach out to help, the other part told her to keep focused on the business at hand. This woman could help Stacy reach her goal, and she seemed eager to become a Beauty Consultant. Yet Stacy was reluctant.

"Suddenly, the husband excused himself. He had to leave for work," recalls Stacy. "I took this as a sign. Now I could broach the fear that I had sensed with the woman."

It was just as Stacy had thought. The woman was indeed in an abusive situation. It was, she confided, a potential powder keg.

They talked for what seemed like hours, heart-to-heart and woman-to-woman.

"I knew that rather than signing up for a Mary Kay career, she needed to go to a shelter for victims of domestic abuse. She needed intervention."

Rather than getting a new team member that day, Stacy got on the phone and got the name of a crisis counselor. Instead of taking the woman to her meeting that night, she took her to get help.

Barbara DeLorimiere

Quality Versus Quantity

*She was especially glad they had
a big group coming when she
learned that Mary Kay Ash had
chartered a plane to get to
Abilene in time for the workshop.*

*I*t was her first year as an Independent Beauty Consultant, and Barbara DeLorimiere was given the honor of driving Mary Kay from the airport to the meeting.

Barbara felt that Mary Kay had freed her from 10 years, as she says, "of being confined to a cage" – a teller's cage at the bank, where she stood all day and never saw sunlight or walked outside from morning until night.

She was anxious to soak up as much from Mary Kay as she could. In every conversation they would have for the next 30 years, Barbara says Mary Kay shared her wisdom – whether about the business or about life in general.

That day, however, when Barbara excitedly told Mary Kay how many were attending the Mary Kay workshop, she got an answer she never anticipated, nor ever will forget.

"I was so excited because we had over 100 women at the meeting. Now, this was no small feat for a Mary Kay workshop in Abilene, Texas, in the early days of our Company," says Barbara. "I thought having 125 people would assure that Mary Kay felt this trip was worth her while."

Mary Kay's response stunned her.

"Barbara, having just 25 at the workshop would be much better than 125," said Mary Kay, and she proceeded to teach Barbara a personal lesson about motivating people.

"She explained to me her philosophy that it is easier to teach in a small group where you can reach people one-on-one. That's what she has always taught. Mary Kay believes motivation comes individually, not collectively or in large groups."

Barbara says she also learned from Mary Kay her philosophy about bringing new people into the business. As Mary Kay once advised, "When you are thinking of asking someone to join your team, think if you would like to have her in your home or to share a hotel room with her."

Pam Gruber

Pam, We Have A Problem

*They were seated next to each
other at the very back of the room.
She doesn't know how she saw it.
All she knows is that Mary Kay
sensed a problem in row seven.*

$\mathcal{M}$ary Kay's visit to the United Kingdom was for the first
Seminar in London. Pam Gruber's experience there has
helped her truly appreciate the elaborate preparations taken
prior to every Mary Kay special event to ensure that all
those deserving recognition receive it. An entire department
is charged with event recognition, and they work tirelessly
to ensure Mary Kay's standard is met: zero tolerance for
leaving someone out.

Down to the person, Mary Kay doesn't want anyone left out.
Even if they're the only ones who know it.

The new British subsidiary wasn't very large, so in their
recognition the meeting planners included as many
categories as possible in order to recognize the group's
success. Pam was one of the U.S. sales force members asked
to help plan the event.

"Mary Kay told me she wanted to sit in the back of the
room so that we could watch the event progress and see all
the excitement in the room," Pam recalls. All was going very
well, or so Pam thought.

In the midst of the recognition, Mary Kay nudged Pam and
said, "About seven rows down from the front and five seats
in, I believe we have a problem. Would you go inquire."

Pam hadn't noticed a problem, but she agreed to proceed
to row seven. Sure enough, one of the Independent Beauty
Consultants had been left off the list of winners in a
category. Pam notified the master of ceremonies and the
mistake was corrected.

Later, Pam quizzed Mary Kay.

"How did you know? How could you see from where we sat and I couldn't?"

Mary Kay explained that she'd learned to read body language – even from the back.

"I know how much a little recognition can mean to a woman. It's so important that we show our people that we care and we understand how much it means to be recognized for their achievements. That's how we grow Beauty Consultants into National Sales Directors."

SuzAnne Brothers

A Marathon, Not a Sprint

*She thought she was something pretty
special as she stood onstage having
achieved $950,000 in unit retail
sales that year, up from $750,000
the year prior and $450,000
the year before that.*

"Mary Kay approached me and clasped my hand in hers and looked me squarely in the eye for what seemed like forever."

In those precious moments, SuzAnne Brothers' life flashed before her and she was thinking how smart she was to have brought her unit this far. She was hoping that she looked as great as she felt on that stage at that moment. She was eagerly anticipating the words her beloved mentor was about to utter. She was prepared to blush and be humble even though she was feeling like the queen of the world.

And then Mary Kay whispered in her ear.

"You should have done a million."

Mary Kay's words froze in SuzAnne's mind. She was speechless. And in that instant, SuzAnne knew Mary Kay was right. That brief encounter became a learning "paycheck" that took SuzAnne all the way to the top of the business.

"There are defining moments in our careers. For me, this was that moment," says SuzAnne, who is convinced that her success leading up to her debut as a National Sales Director in 1995 was due completely to taking Mary Kay's admonishment and making good on it.

"Believe it or not," SuzAnne says, "those words made me realize that there are times when a leader must pull out all the stops in going for a goal. All year we had worked on doing a million. I stopped short – $50,000 short."

SuzAnne had always listened to Mary Kay's teachings, but the best thing about this lesson in leadership was that Mary Kay didn't worry about how Suzanne might take it.

"Mary Kay has always said that this career is a marathon and not a sprint. But after that year, I understood that sometimes you must pull out all the stops and go for the team goal."

"And to do that, you have to sprint."

Donna Floberg

Mary Kay Is In Me

*She just had to see for herself
if she really wanted to sell this stuff.*

That's why Donna Floberg drove six hours to a meeting where Mary Kay Ash was the guest.

"I thought if she didn't look good when I got up close to her, I would have my answer. I wouldn't want to sell her cosmetics," says Donna.

When Donna finally made her way to the front of the receiving line, she got her answer. And she got something else she hadn't bargained for.

"At the time I only wanted to earn $50 to buy my husband a present without spending his money. That was my total motivation."

But Mary Kay had other plans. Donna could see up close that this was a beautiful woman. And Mary Kay could see a potential in Donna far beyond any Donna saw in herself. Mary Kay said, "I want to see you in Dallas."

Donna said she was planning to attend that year's Seminar.

"No," said Mary Kay, "I want you to come to Dallas qualified to be a Sales Director."

"Something snapped," Donna recalls. "Mary Kay believed in me and suddenly I began believing in myself. I was the woman who couldn't even decide what to order in a restaurant without checking with my husband first!"

In that instant, Donna not only was in Mary Kay; Mary Kay also was "in" Donna. She did come to Dallas a year later, debuting as a record-breaking Sales Director.

And the story could come to a close right there. But it was in sharing the opportunity that Donna got her greatest "paycheck."

Penny was an enthusiastic enough guest. Donna just wasn't in the habit yet of asking her customers if they were interested in hearing more about this career. Shortly after having that personal visit with Mary Kay, something made Donna call Penny to check her interest.

Penny's answer shocked Donna.

"She said she'd wanted to ask me about the career after attending my class, but she couldn't bring herself to say anything because her self-esteem was so low. Penny told me she had recently lost her 10-year-old son to a heart attack, and her entire family was grieving, depressed and angry.

"I thank God I asked her," says Donna, who has had the pleasure of watching Penny grow in her career, help her family heal and teach hundreds of women to achieve their potential. Penny has earned the use of eight pink cars.

Nancy Sullivan

She Only Had Eyes for Me

David didn't have to be convinced this was a great opportunity for his wife.

She had already searched all over New Hampshire for someone who sold the brand of skin care that had improved her cousin's skin so dramatically. Nancy Sullivan wanted to buy *Mary Kay*® products so badly that she extended her search into Boston, where she finally found a Beauty Consultant.

"I called her and asked her to send the entire collection. She insisted on bringing it to my house so she could teach me how to use it properly," says Nancy, who had the money sitting out on the table so she wouldn't need to spend more time than necessary.

David was curious enough that he came home for lunch. The first thing he noticed was that this Sales Director was wearing a "$3,000" pin. When she told David that it signified her monthly commissions, he really sat up and took notice.

It wasn't long before Nancy had become a Beauty Consultant herself.

David never had any problem supporting his wife's growth in her Mary Kay career, especially after one particularly meaningful conversation when Mary Kay Ash showed him the amazing power of "make me feel important."

"Anwar Sadat and George Bush both could have been standing there and Mary Kay wouldn't have seen either of them," David recalls of his meeting with Mary Kay. He was standing at the elevator lobby of the Fairmont Hotel in Dallas when Mary Kay recognized him as being the husband of a new Sales Director.

The two conversed for at least 10 minutes. Each time the elevator doors opened there were hordes of Sales Directors and Beauty Consultants who could hardly contain their excitement at seeing their founder. David, meanwhile, was thinking, surely most of these people were more important than he was.

"I knew she could hear those same 'Irish whispers' I was hearing," David recalls, "but Mary Kay never glanced left or right. She kept her gaze fixed intently on me as we talked.

"She only had eyes for me, and did that ever make me feel important!"

Fran Cikalo

Trophy on Wheels

*When she was a little girl growing
up on Clark Street in the shadow of the
General Motors Cadillac division
in Detroit, Fran Cikalo used to sit on
her front porch and watch as new
Cadillacs were driven off the plant docks.*

"I thought as a child that driving a Cadillac must be the epitome of success, that you had to be really good and really rich to drive one," recalls Fran, a first generation American whose immigrant parents spoke only broken English.

Fran went on to the University of Michigan where she majored in engineering. It was only after living the suburban good life with a happy marriage, three children and a four-bedroom home far from the neighborhood of her youth that Fran decided to pursue her own youthful dreams of making something of herself.

"Like so many women, my identity was tied up in that of my husband and my children. I'd lost a lot of the confidence of my youth. I needed to find my own self-worth."

Fran started her Mary Kay business and she advanced in her career. By 1979, she was driving a pink Cadillac. Because of that, she had a once-in-a-lifetime opportunity provided for her by Mary Kay that is still the most defining moment of her life.

After Mary Kay learned that Fran had grown up living in the shadow of the Cadillac plant in Detroit, she hatched a plan in her typical Cinderella style.

She arranged for Fran to accompany her on a 1984 visit to the Cadillac plant. This wasn't just any visit. Fran and Mary Kay would be driven – in a Cadillac limousine – past her childhood home, rolling proudly down her old street right up into the Cadillac assembly line!

"It was the most wonderful moment of my life. It was like living a dream fulfilled. I must say I felt really good and really rich that day! But more important, by Mary Kay's reminder of how far I'd come, I had gotten back my self-worth. Many have called our pink Cadillac a trophy on wheels. It was that and so much more for me."

Fran's Cinderella day didn't stop there. Mary Kay also planned a special luncheon in the executive suite at Cadillac where Fran was reunited with one of her most successful University of Michigan engineering classmates – the former president of Cadillac.

"Talk about Mary Kay's philosophy of 'make me feel important'. I am living proof that it works."

Kathy Rasmussen

A Legacy of Caring

Possibility thinking was something that came naturally to Julie. After all, she'd spent her entire life around some of the most charismatic women leaders of Mary Kay – including her own mother, Kathy Rasmussen.

When Julie Rasmussen was named general manager of Mary Kay Russia, she had impeccable college credentials, a gift for languages and solid work experiences abroad. However, it was Julie's perspective on what the Company could do for the women of Russia that really excited Mary Kay Ash.

She told Mary Kay of her impressions of having worked for an American company in Russia. She shared with Mary Kay her dream for bringing *this* American company to the women of Russia.

Her mother recalls the conversation and Julie's passionate words to Mary Kay:

"We'd be able to get the women off the streets. It's a very matriarchal society – women do all the menial jobs like digging ditches and cleaning the streets. This career opportunity is one of the greatest gifts we could ever provide them. Mary Kay, we have a chance to help an entire nation of women here."

The message hit home with Mary Kay.

Mary Kay spoke of the conversation in a speech some years later when she related how so often those interviewing for a position in the international division would want to impress the founder by discussing how much money they were going to make.

"Julie," said Mary Kay, "told me how many lives we were going to touch."

Today, Julie Rasmussen is the president of Mary Kay Europe.

Carmen Ríos

Proven Priorities

*She has lived Mary Kay priorities of
God first, family second and career third.
It nearly cost her the career
she loved so much.*

By 1984, Carmen Ríos had progressed to the status of
Independent Senior Sales Director, driving her first pink
Cadillac and achieving other top honors in her native
Puerto Rico.

She received word late that year that her sister, who lived in
the United States, had acquired AIDS. Carmen was the only
one in the family with the flexibility and the finances to
make the trip to see about her sister's health, so off she went.

In putting her family before her career during this crisis, Carmen was forced to give up the use of the Cadillac she had worked so hard to earn. She went from being one of the top Independent Sales Directors to nearly losing her position as a Sales Director.

"There were times it seemed that only God was on my side," she observes today. "And then I would remember Mary Kay was also on my side."

Following her sister's death, Carmen felt she was testing Mary Kay priorities when she decided to resume working her business. She was skeptical but willing to start over if that's what it would take for her to again achieve success. Almost miraculously, the business began to grow again. But this time it was even stronger than before.

Six months later, Carmen had earned the use of another Cadillac and her name began reappearing on the top Sales Directors' lists.

"The second time around the blessings were even greater than before. I had followed our priorities to put my family before my career, and what I gained in the balance was the prestigious status of National Sales Director."

Mary Diem

The Real Draw

Since she was very young, she had always gravitated toward being in the company of strong women. Now she has an entire company of strong women from whom to draw strength.

Mary Diem admits she might have forgotten two of the most important perks of her Mary Kay career if it weren't for two things that happened recently to point out to her what is so obviously the greatest "paycheck" of this career. That is, says Mary, "Being your own boss and being a part of a very supportive network of women."

The first realization came from Mary's mom, who receives the Preferred Customer Program mailings. "I got a call from my mother after she had read some of the material that the Company sends out to my customers. It's sent with my name on it.

"I've been a National Sales Director for five years now and with Mary Kay for more than 20 years, but Mom has never really understood what it is I do. After reading some of the brochures she was sent, Mom called and said, 'You must be so excited now that you are your own boss.' Finally, after 20 years, she understood!"

Mary was recently reminded of another reward when she was visiting with some of her area Sales Directors, and they began talking about the collective strength of the Mary Kay family.

"We are so much like a family and so close."

The Sales Directors were lamenting the fact that four of the group had battled cancer and two had lost their battle. The day before her death, one of the women was visiting with a sister Sales Director. She made the comment that she wished she had shared the Mary Kay opportunity with more women.

"It reminded me," says Mary, "of the quote I've heard that 'when you are near the end, you never say "I wish I'd spent more time at work."'"

" This is probably the only business in the world where someone would wish that she'd spent more time on her business. It's because of this wonderful sisterhood that the camaraderie becomes so much a part of your being."

Charlene Bourne

Pampered and Fluffed

*There hadn't been much
correlation between
looking good on the outside
and feeling better on the inside
when Mary Kay agreed to
participate in a fun experiment.*

After she saw the results of the program she began in the early days of the Company to send volunteers into nursing homes armed with skin care and glamour products, she spread the word with her sales force nationwide. Charlene Bourne was one of those who heeded her call.

She initiated a weekly program for any of the Mary Kay Independent Sales Directors and Beauty Consultants living in Tucson who wanted to donate their time. The Company donated the products. Just as they do in skin care classes, the volunteers taught the nursing home residents application techniques and beauty tips that they could do themselves.

"We saw how much it meant to the women when we'd give them the chance to try everything. At first, we didn't think at their ages they'd want too much color in their glamour products, but we soon saw that blue was the favorite eye shadow color," says Charlene.

It wasn't long before "pampered and fluffed" day, as the residents called it, became the event residents and staff looked forward to the most. "You can't imagine how it felt to walk into a nursing home and have so many people excited to see you. And to have all your time booked." The men, says Charlene, looked forward to these days as well. Flirting certainly increased!

Along with the beauty secrets, Charlene added a little Mary Kay enthusiasm. The group would sing, clap and recognize every resident in some small way.

But something else happened on the way to fulfilling these elderly women's dreams.

Charlene's business had been great, but now it started booming. Without even realizing it she was achieving much more than she ever imagined. "The program just caught on fire, and others in the community could see that we had something very special to offer women. The opportunity to help our neighbors and friends was something Mary Kay encouraged from the beginning."

Charlene called Mary Kay to express amazement.

"I'm not surprised at all. You took care of a very special part of this business. And now this business is taking care of you. It is very true that all you send into the lives of others comes back into your own," Mary Kay said.

Martha Langford

VisionLand

Since he retired as head of the FBI
in their hometown, her husband
helped develop and serves as General
Manager of a new family theme
park called VisionLand.

But it's Martha Langford who believes she's been the one living in a land of great vision since 1973. Martha's experience is that Mary Kay has always seen farther than others see. What Mary Kay saw first, she has communicated beautifully to others.

Martha loved the product the first time she tried it, but she came to a deep and abiding respect for Mary Kay's philosophy above everything.

Martha believes she has had a full course in what she calls God's finishing school for women. "Mary Kay uses the living, sculpting tools of praise and encouragement. She shared a good head for business and an even bigger heart.

"She once told me that my role as a leader was to nurture the seeds of greatness in every woman. She asked only that each of us encourage them and love them. She said the only way they would fail would be if they just quit.

" 'If you make a mistake, we just pick you up, dust you off and tell you how beautifully you fell.' This is a wonderful constant we can offer to others. We fall forward to success. It is a vision that will always continue."

Gloria Castaño
More Than Decoration

She didn't set out to change a culture;
she just knew she wanted more.

When she thinks how many woman are still sitting at home "with their music left unplayed," as Mary Kay says, Gloria Castaño is so very proud that she refused to be silent.

She would never have had to go to work. She could have easily spent her days devoted to very satisfying charity work. It was, in fact, assumed that women of her station in life would find total fulfillment in this way. When she left her comfortable surroundings in Colombia, Gloria knew she was seeking personal growth more than anything. A career would have been out of the question in Colombia.

"I was bored. I always knew I wanted more."

Gloria reflects after 20 years since her move – one so bold that her brothers still don't grasp it two decades later. Still, she knows that in her own small way, she did "change the concept" of what was acceptable for an entire family.
"I refused to be a decoration," she declares.

Because of that, Gloria's own daughter, as well as her nieces and cousins, face a life that will allow many choices. "They will never be expected to be happy being a piece of art.

"They will seek balance in a world that has finally come to see it as good. I strongly emphasize that the priorities need to be lived in the order that Mary Kay Ash said: God first, family second and career third.

"What a positive influence. How joyful and nurturing that Mary Kay embraces women of any culture.

"As our gift, we must leave in her name our own legacy of inspirational deeds."

Wisdom

"I believe that everyone

who accomplishes

something great

had help from someone.

Somebody, somewhere

provided a spark

of inspiration, offered

a challenge or held

out a hand

along the way."

Kerry Buskirk

A Moment for Mom

*The woman looked like a character
out of a Disney fable. She was
dressed in overalls and her long gray
hair dangled unruly below her waist.*

She certainly didn't fit in with the others attending the
meeting in the small Kansas town. But she'd been brought as
a guest to a meeting Kerry Buskirk was hosting, and Kerry
recalled Mary Kay's teaching that she should always treat
every guest with respect. She also recalled Mary Kay saying
that we should never prejudge based on outward
appearances.

Even though it was a reach, Kerry was cordial.

The woman's daughter was one of Kerry's good customers who enjoyed hosting skin care classes. Kerry recalls, however, that everything she wore was basically "too short, too tight and too revealing." So before inviting this customer to the event at which she was honoring her best hostesses, Kerry had carefully explained to her that dress for the evening was "professional" and she hoped for the best. She also told the woman she could bring a guest.

The customer came dressed as conservatively as Kerry had ever seen her. She told Kerry she'd bought a new scarf and hat for the event. She also brought her mother along because Kerry had told the customer she was being recognized as "top hostess" that month. The mother was the one with waist-length gray hair who was dressed in faded overalls.

When time came for the recognition, Kerry said something nice about each hostess. She watched as tears streamed down the mother's face when her daughter's name was called, and her scruffy appearance melted into that of smiling and proud mom.

Kerry didn't have any contact with this customer for several months after that evening, but one day she called to tell

Kerry that her mom had died. She also had another message, a "paycheck of the heart" spoken haltingly, but sincerely.

"At your meeting, when I was recognized as a top hostess, it was a very special occasion for my mother. No one in my family has ever done much of anything besides get in trouble. I have two brothers in prison, and you probably know I work as an exotic dancer. I brought my mom to your meeting so she could see all the nice ladies.

"That evening was the first and only time in my mom's entire life that she ever had any reason to be proud of any of her kids. She told me it was the proudest night of her life, and she was happy to know that I might find a better way of life by associating with nice people like you."

Elizabeth Fitzpatrick

"God's Delay Is Not God's Denial"

*As she stood onstage that day surrounded
by the three most important women
in her life, she finally understood
what Mary Kay had been telling
her all those years.*

As the daughter of one of the most successful National
Sales Directors ever, Elizabeth Fitzpatrick had already quit the
career several times. At the age of 18 and also at 22, Elizabeth
had tried the career only to find the timing wasn't right.

"It wasn't easy being the daughter of the No. 1 NSD in
Mary Kay. Anything short of her success was my failure,"
Elizabeth recalls. Mary Kay Ash had encouraged Elizabeth

to remember she was unique and talented, and she also reminded her that no one could aspire to the status of National without earning it – no matter who her mother was.

By the time she was 28, Elizabeth, then a single mom, had become an Executive Senior Sales Director earning a six-figure income. She considered quitting the business because, again, the pressure to measure up to her mother's success was getting to her.

It was then that Elizabeth's mom, NSD Emeritus Shirley Hutton, intervened, begging her daughter to realize how few careers offer a working mother balance between work and family.

"Stay where you are and quit worrying about what I think," Shirley told Elizabeth.

By 1993, Elizabeth was ready to qualify for National Sales Director when she ended up in bed for four months. She was pregnant and had kidney stones that were inoperable.

Again, Mary Kay and Shirley worked to convince Elizabeth she could still fulfill her destiny as a National. "I doubted them both at the time," Elizabeth recalls. However, there was something Mary Kay said that stuck with her.

It was: "God's delay is not God's denial."

Fifteen months later, she stood onstage at a Mary Kay Seminar holding her baby daughter, Konnar, along with a beaming Mary Kay Ash and a justifiably proud Shirley Hutton. It is a moment Elizabeth will not soon forget. "The three most important women in my life were there with me to celebrate my success.

"I finally understood."

Rosa Jackson

One-Liners of a Lifetime

So often, all it would take for her
to understand was to hear one
of Mary Kay's legendary one-liners.

*T*here are so many of them sprinkled through Rosa
Jackson's career that she cannot possibly name just one
"paycheck." But when pressed, she can narrow it down
to three.

Rosa finds it fitting that, although she has a master's degree
in Christian education, it was Mary Kay Ash who instantly
set Rosa's priorities straight early in her career. Mary Kay's
advice moved her – literally and spiritually – when she
balked at the idea of having to relocate with her husband
just as her business was taking off. Mary Kay said:

"It is no fun counting money by yourself. Go with Lewis to Texas knowing that the same God that helped you in Atlanta will be there in Houston."

On another occasion when Mary Kay learned that Rosa's generosity had been taken advantage of by someone who never paid Rosa back the product she had borrowed, Mary Kay said, "Resist the temptation to be a missionary. The way to really help these women is to teach them how to gather their own strength and run their own business. You must help them learn that one can never do business out of an empty wagon."

Finally, there was the time years ago when Rosa and every other member of the Mary Kay independent sales force in Atlanta were eagerly preparing to greet Mary Kay at the airport. They'd been told that Mary Kay loved children, so entire families came to greet her plane.

Rosa's daughter, Rosalynn, was only five at the time. She was standing in the reception area. Mary Kay's late husband Mel, a man with a rugged complexion, came down the concourse first and he greeted everyone fondly. He was followed by Mary Kay, who spotted Rosalynn and reached down to hug her.

"Mary Kay," said the little girl, "your husband must not use OUR products."

"I wanted to faint and disappear into the floor," says Rosa.

But Mary Kay replied without missing a beat, "Oh, precious, you know how these menfolks are!"

With her usual aplomb, Mary Kay had saved a potentially embarrassing situation. Later, she and Rosa shared a hearty laugh. Mary Kay, recalls Rosa, was impressed that Rosalynn referred to them as "our" products!

Pat Danforth

Five Minutes on Life

*In any Mary Kay appearance,
Pat Danforth is committed to
speaking at least five minutes on
something that has nothing to do
with cosmetics or the opportunity.*

$\mathcal{T}$he gist of the message is: "Take care of yourself. Be responsible for yourself." Pat Danforth strongly believes that self-confidence and a positive attitude can make a difference in handling any of life's situations. She is certain that she would not be here today had it not been for the constant messages she received from Mary Kay Ash about women and cancer.

When a yearly mammogram indicated a mass in her breast, Pat had a subsequent ultrasound that was interpreted as "OK." Knowing she exhibited the warning signs of cancer, Pat kept pursuing a more accurate diagnosis. A biopsy was done and the results came back "malignant."

Because of her faith and her Mary Kay education, Pat knew that she was strong enough and well prepared to fight. Remarkably, she faced a very aggressive cancer and came to the acceptance stage, as she says, "Without going through the usual stages of shock, denial and anger beforehand." From the beginning, Pat faced her cancer with the attitude: "All right, what are we going to do about this?"

With that, Pat set off on a cancer-fighting course that would find her looking like she just stepped out of *Vogue* through the several surgeries, chemotherapy, radiation and various complications that would ensue. Throughout these challenges people would comment, "But you look so good."

"Looking good was my best defense," Pat recalls. "Mary Kay always impressed upon us the importance of *looking our best* so that we could *be our best*. I firmly believe that. My hair and eyelashes might be gone, I may have had tubes attached to me, my hand and arm might be swollen – but I was going to do my best not to look sick."

Pat believes it was her faith, her family and her Mary Kay attitude that provided the difference that helped the doctors treat her successfully. She also believes the cancer experience strengthened all these aspects of her life.

Today, Pat feels compelled to share this message and this strength with others. "My years with Mary Kay helped give me the tools to fight this disease. Mary Kay would expect me to share my experience in the hope it will help others."

Barbara Faber

The Meeting

*She knew that as a future
Independent National Sales Director,
she would have the special opportunity
to visit with the Company founder.*

*B*arbara Faber just never realized how special the meeting would be. Or that she would be among the last of the up-and-coming NSDs to savor this moment that only 100 women before her had experienced.

Barbara had imagined many times how the meeting would be. As she walked that day to the hotel suite where she had been invited to meet with Mary Kay Ash, Barbara expected it would be the way it is in the movies when someone goes to visit a famous person.

"I imagined that an assistant would answer the doorbell and that I would be escorted to a sitting area to wait for Mary Kay to come and greet me. I thought it would all be very formal. I assumed there would be someone checking the time to make sure I didn't overstay my visit."

It was very different from what Barbara had envisioned.

Mary Kay herself answered the door. The sight of that famous loving smile greeting her at the door literally took Barbara's breath away.

For the next hour, the two talked woman-to-woman about Mary Kay philosophies and priorities.

"No matter how big we get," Mary Kay said, "I want you to be very clear that it is the job of you and your sister NSDs to give our philosophies top priority."

Barbara left the meeting that day firm in her belief that Mary Kay had given her this meaningful message for a reason. She wasn't to understand the significance until six months later when she learned that Mary Kay had suffered a stroke that robbed her of her voice.

"She had so poignantly explained to me that day the importance of continuing her dream. She talked about us Nationals being her voice and passing her message on."

Since that meeting, Barbara has a much deeper understanding of what it is to keep alive and build upon the foundation that Mary Kay built. The meeting and, more important, the message, will forever hold a special place in her heart.

Marlys Skillings

Take Time to Know

She was seated next to Mary Kay
at a special luncheon when she
learned a lesson that would impact
the remainder of her career.

Marlys Skillings had been a model and a television talk show host before deciding to become an Independent Beauty Consultant. Both of her former careers were "me" centered, so Marlys has always been grateful for a lesson she learned at her very first Seminar.

"As the emcee announced the names of that year's contest winners, he mispronounced several names. Not wanting to embarrass him, Mary Kay whispered the correct pronunciations under her breath and then she turned to me," Marlys recalls.

Mary Kay said, "It is so important to take the time to make sure you know the name and how to pronounce it so you can give people the recognition they deserve."

Marlys learned from Mary Kay that no detail is too small for her attention. Mary Kay also taught her that no matter how successful we become, we should always remember those who helped us along the way.

"This has been the best 'paycheck' of my career because it taught me about focusing attention on others rather than myself. It showed me that being others-focused rather than me-focused earns so much more love and respect and, in the end, success."

Johnnette Shealy

My She-ro (aka He-ro!)

Mary Kay did more to liberate more women than any other woman in American history. But she was no women's libber.

She didn't like it when the women's movement urged women to begin acting more masculine – in their dress, demeanor and language.

Mary Kay called a girl a girl even when it wasn't cool. She was thinking like a woman when some clearly were not. Her favorite expression upon learning that one of her Sales Directors had extremely high earnings was: "Now that is girl-sized pay!"

"We don't have to burn our bras to make a point," she said to anyone who'd listen.

Johnnette Shealy was listening. This devoted wife and mother had begun to question her life and wonder where she would be in the next 10 years. Mary Kay's voice struck a chord deep within her.

"There were two voices speaking inside me. One was this doubting twerp telling me I should just be satisfied with being a wife and mother – that I could never succeed at a career. The other voice was saying: You are strong, you are invincible, you can do anything."

Mary Kay's message was the first one that gave women like Johnnette permission to think they could do anything. "She gave us permission to dream again – to dream big and to focus on growing together with examples set by all these other women.

"It was the first time I heard about women working together for the good of everyone. Sharing our strength made so much sense to me," says Johnnette.

After Johnnette became a Mary Kay Beauty Consultant, she received something else she never could have anticipated.

"The first applause since my wedding. The first awards since high school graduation. The first recognition of my accomplishments ever in my life occurred the first time I walked onto that Seminar stage," Johnnette recalls.

As she walked onto that stage nervous and unsure about her future, Mary Kay Ash was there to greet her.

"She didn't know me, but she somehow must have known what I was thinking. She took my hands and looked into my eyes with a spirited and sincere gleam in her clear blue eyes and she told me: 'You can do it.'

"I did it. I believed her. Leaning into her dream brought my own dream to fruition."

Jo Anne Cunnington
Face the Fear

*By the time she had gotten to the
head table at this important
banquet, she had already experienced
more pain than most people
will in a lifetime.*

*N*one of the 3,000 people in the ballroom could even have
imagined the conversation going on at the head table
between Jo Anne Cunnington and Mary Kay Ash. Jo Anne
didn't realize it at the time, but it wasn't just happenstance
that Mary Kay was seated next to her.

Even though she was at the top of career, she was in the
depths of depression in her personal life. This night,
Mary Kay took it as her personal challenge to change that.

"Mary Kay was never content for us to be just good business women. She wants us to be good at everything – including motherhood and role modeling, not to mention our marriages. That night, she told me that I needed to let go of my pain and get on with my life. She said I must begin to look forward, not back. She said if I could do that for one week, I could do it forever."

The two women sat at the banquet holding hands; both had tears running down their cheeks. "Mary Kay was never afraid to use her own life as an example if she thought it could help us. She told me about the painful divorce from the father of her children. She explained how she had looked forward to his coming home from overseas, but that when he did, he announced he didn't want to be married anymore."

Mary Kay described it as the lowest point of her life. "Jo Anne, on that day I felt like a complete and total failure. Nothing had ever struck me so hard," Mary Kay tenderly said.

It was also the time, she said, that she had to face the fact that now she would have to do the thing that women of her generation feared the most: raise and provide for her children as a single mother.

"Mary Kay helped me realize that night that it was time for me to do some more growing in order to make better decisions in my personal life. She explained that when our self-esteem is low, we make poor choices. Mary Kay has always made me want to grow. She makes you believe you have it inside of you."

Sonya Gregian

"She Saw Something In Me I Couldn't See"

*After holding seven jobs
in 14 years, Sonya Gregian
admits she was happy just
plodding along, willing to settle
for what others would pay her.*

That was before she met Mary Kay Ash in February 1975 at a class in New York City.

"I took down every word she said. Mary Kay must have noticed because after the class she came over to me, put her arms around me and asked when I expected to become an Independent Sales Director."

It had already taken Sonya six months to get her business off the ground, so she figured she'd give Mary Kay a safe answer – six more months, August.

Mary Kay looked at Sonya and she shook her head.

"No. Sooner," she told the now terrified Independent Beauty Consultant.

"July?" asked Sonya. And Mary Kay shook her head again.

Her answers: "June?" and "May?" got the same response.

Almost afraid to utter the word, Sonya blurted out, "April?" – six weeks away – to which Mary Kay finally nodded yes!

"Is she crazy?" Sonya recalls thinking.

Back at home, Sonya received a personal note from Mary Kay.

"She had reserved me a place in the new Sales Directors class! She explained that she saw something in me that she knew I couldn't see in myself," Sonya recalls today.

"If she hadn't expected this of me, I don't think I or anyone else in my life would have."

Sonya lived up to Mary Kay's expectations. She was in the April class, and three months later she became a Sales Director.

Mary Kay told Sonya years later there was no way she was going to give a sharp woman like Sonya permission to slack off. "She told me I'd be wise to provide that kind of development for my own area Sales Directors. She explained that all she did was to instill a sense of urgency in me that had never existed before."

"She saw something in me I couldn't yet see. Isn't that the true mark of a leader?"

Alia Head

The Only Bible That Some Will Ever Read

It was affirmation that
she had made the right choice.

*A*lia Head had prepared herself to become a lawyer by majoring in pre-law in college and working for law firms. She had already been accepted to law school when she had a change of heart about pursuing her chosen profession.

So it was that when the time came for Alia to have her future Independent National Sales Director interview with Mary Kay Ash, she came prepared with questions.

The answers she got were both an illustration of Mary Kay's character and a full endorsement for Alia that she had made the right choice when she selected the Mary Kay career over one in law.

"It was the first time I was completely alone with her. It will always be my best memory and one of the most special blessings of this career," Alia recalls of the meeting that took place in Mary Kay's office.

Alia, who had met her husband in a church class for singles, respected Mary Kay's commitment to the priorities of God first, family second and career third. In their meeting, Alia asked Mary Kay for her wisdom on the link between career and faith.

Mary Kay's simple and profound answer was:

"I found that the best way to share was simply to tell stories of how the Lord has worked in my life. And then to strive to live in a way that reflects that faith."

Mary Kay continued, "You, Alia, are the only Bible that some people will ever read."

Joyce Grady

My Name is Joyce

Although she had traveled on the top
Sales Director trip to London in the
company of Mary Kay Ash, she still felt
compelled to introduce herself in case
Mary Kay didn't remember who she was.

"I didn't realize at the time that Mary Kay prides herself on remembering people's names. She is phenomenal. Throughout my entire career I've always been so in awe of this woman. I've tried to mold my life after hers."

But Joyce Grady refused to believe that someone as important as Mary Kay actually knew her name even this time, as they were seated next to each other at a grand finale dinner. Mary Kay spoke to the crowd telling them how special they were and how much she enjoyed being with each of them.

As the evening was coming to a close, Joyce summoned all her courage. She introduced herself and asked Mary Kay to sign her menu from the gala evening. Mary Kay crooked her head and looked at Joyce.

"I will only sign your menu if you promise me that you will not feel as if you ever have to tell me your name again!"

She never did. It was a defining moment.

There is yet another moment Joyce believes defines the real "paycheck" of her career.

Joyce's sister, Janice, had lost her 24-year-old son just weeks before she was slated to speak at a Mary Kay Seminar – one of the greatest honors in Janice's life. She called Joyce for advice on what to do.

"Janice was relieved that the Company reached out to her in compassion and never for a minute expected her to speak after what she'd been through. But, still, my sister felt she needed to go on. She felt she needed to speak because she had a story to tell."

Janice told her story that day at Seminar. She recalled how years before her sister, Joyce, had begun to experience success as a Mary Kay Beauty Consultant. Joyce had saved money to attend an event in Philadelphia which Mary Kay had been expected to attend. As it turned out, the event happened so soon after the death of her husband, Mel, that no one really expected she would attend – and she certainly wouldn't speak if she did come.

Joyce had impressed upon her sister many times how Mary Kay's example that day ignited her own passion in this career. "I never could have known it would do the same for my sister," Joyce says. "Our own first lady had every reason to make an excuse that day. But she didn't. It was very painful for her to stand before thousands of adoring members of the sales force with her grief and her pain so fresh.

"But Mary Kay did it anyway."

And so did Janice.

Míriam Gómez-Rivas

A Chip Off the Old Block

*She has learned that life is
truly what happens while you are
busy making other plans.*

*T*he same year she opened her successful clothing
boutique in Puerto Rico, Míriam Gómez-Rivas also decided
to dabble in Mary Kay. Soon she was earning much more
than she ever imagined from her "dabbling" – and more than
that, she had developed a passion that would not go away.

Míriam was afraid to let her husband know how much she
loved Mary Kay because he had made a large investment in
her boutique. But her husband sensed Míriam's passion for
the Mary Kay career and advised her to sell the boutique.

She will never forget the feeling that day – "like a bird newly freed from a cage!"

Míriam's unit went on to become the first million-dollar unit in Puerto Rico, and she became the first Independent Sales Director of Dominican heritage.

Although the situation is quite different, Míriam watches today as another young woman struggles with the same dilemmas she did just 15 years ago.

A woman named Diana chips away at her $84,000 student loan debt with earnings from her Mary Kay career. Diana is beginning to see the same thing her mentor saw: that the business she started to help her get out of debt may soon overtake the goal she had to become a Doctor of Optometry. She's feeling torn between the career she struggled so hard to achieve and the one that allowed her to achieve it.

Although she realized her dream of becoming an optometrist and is currently practicing her profession, Diana's struggle is not lost on Míriam. She shudders to think what might have become of her life if she'd given up Mary Kay instead of the boutique.

"Whatever the outcome, I also know that Diana realizes she's just one of the many women who've had the course of their life changed by the Mary Kay opportunity."

Nancy Tietjen

And She Lived Happily Ever After...

*The end of the fairy tale where the
princess rides off into the sunset
with the handsome prince was the part
that she always loved reading to her girls.*

Although Nancy Tietjen trudged through her graveyard
shift at a shotgun shell plant in order to provide for her
children, somewhere in the far corners of her mind was
a glimmer of hope, a belief that fairy tales do come true.

The fairy tale for this single mother began when she found
Mary Kay.

Eight months after becoming an Independent Beauty
Consultant, when she had already reached Top 10 ranking,

Nancy got a call from Mary Kay Ash. She asked Nancy to speak in front of 8,000 people.

Nancy protested. She wasn't qualified to speak. What could she tell these women?

"Tell them," Mary Kay said, "you can do it."

"Mary Kay always understood that in order to overcome fear, you must do the things you fear the most."

Mary Kay also understood fairy tales and how they impact a woman's dreams. She must have understood Nancy's, too, because upon her arrival in Dallas, there was Mary Kay waiting to whisk her off into the sunset in a pink Cadillac with heart-shaped windows.

Nancy's fairy tale was finally coming true.

Nancy doesn't remember much of what she said in her speech that day except something like, "Only in America could somebody like me be talking to you. Only in Mary Kay can your hopes and dreams come true."

Nancy rode the power of that moment for 27 years – never once has she not been in the Top 10 in all those years.

Judie McCoy

You Never Know Who is Coming Through the Door

With her college degrees and experiences,
she was educated in everything
but people and love.

The moment she walked into her first meeting, she displayed an incredibly strong will. Judie McCoy wondered if that is what had caused her difficulty in the convent where she'd spent 34 years as a nun. Judie was stunned at first and a little taken aback that anyone could be so forceful. "It was her strong opinions that really got to me," Judie says.

"Here was this beautiful, highly educated woman who would stand up in my cheery, positive meeting and let me know exactly how she felt about what I was saying – or how I was saying it!"

Judie often went home frustrated. One night she prayed for the strength to help this woman. As she pondered how she would help, Judie remembered something she'd heard Mary Kay Ash say:

"You never know who is coming through that door," Mary Kay had said to a group of Sales Directors. Your role as a Sales Director, she had explained, is to find a way to achieve balance and harmony among women from all backgrounds. Mary Kay always expected that her leaders would not judge anyone based on outward appearances or actions.

"Take time to find out what's going on inside the person," Mary Kay had advised.

Judie took on the challenge. She changed her heart and began getting to know the person. What she found was a woman who had been hurt, who needed a home. A woman who had even tried her hand at selling cars after leaving the convent. This newfound Mary Kay career was to become both a way to support herself financially and also a means to discover a tremendous support network.

She began to see the joy in treating others with tenderness. She learned how to express appreciation. She soaked up the discipline it takes to be part of a team. She listened to Judie.

"I would be the one to call her and offer some less abrasive ways of expressing her feelings," says Judie.

Month by month the woman grew. Judie heard love and caring – locked for so long in her heart – expressed for the first time. Judie heard tenderness after her daughter donated blood for the woman's surgery. She watched with great pride as affection developed between the former nun and her Mary Kay associates.

One more woman had learned how to give and receive love.

"And I learned," says Judie, "what a tremendous vehicle we have for helping women in this Mary Kay career."

Sonya LaVay

The Last Person In Line

*All 3,000 people in the ballroom
wanted their photo made with Mary Kay.
She was the last person in line.*

Sonya LaVay's career was exactly one week old. She couldn't possibly have known that once upon a time, this amazing woman had stood in a line about this long to meet the president of the company she had just begun working for.

She would have no idea that by the time she reached the front of the line – with an attitude that had just about taken her out of the line a few minutes before – this woman named Mary Kay would know exactly the right words to say.

Sonya couldn't fathom that Mary Kay took a lesson from the preoccupied manner in which she had been greeted and formed a company based on the principle she learned that night so many years before.

"If I am ever the person they're waiting in line to meet, I will make them feel as if they're the only person in the room."

Now it was Sonya's turn.

"I walked over to Mary Kay, and I told her that I had just recently started my Mary Kay business after having been a district manager for a Mary Kay competitor. I shared with Mary Kay that I had always wanted to meet her and that I thought I could be successful in her company."

Mary Kay took Sonya's hands in her own. "I know you will be successful. I can see it in your eyes."

There are no words, and certainly no value, that Sonya could put on that moment. Her self-esteem soared, as did her resolve to succeed.

"We have no idea the importance of one-on-one communication. We never know what another person's belief in us can do. That kind of positive reinforcement can have life-changing effects," says Sonya.

"In my career, I have tried to focus my attention on people who come to meet me in the same way that Mary Kay did. I work very hard never to give the idea that I am hurried. I practice it still to this day whether it is the first person, or the last one, in line."

Nancy Bonner

Go Home and Make It Happen

It was the Cinderella lifestyle
that attracted her to
Mary Kay in the first place.

She had already learned that the recognition and the Cinderella prizes were for real, but Nancy Bonner was too busy raising her family, working part of the time as a hairstylist and spending the other time as an Independent Beauty Consultant.

She hadn't thought of becoming a Sales Director. "I loved every minute of being a Beauty Consultant. I had done well enough that I could qualify to attend the 'future' Sales

Directors meetings. I couldn't see myself as Sales Director material, but I did enjoy attending those fun meetings. I guess I must have attended one too many when Mary Kay stopped me at the door one year."

Nancy was nearly seven months pregnant with her third of four sons at the time. She figured Mary Kay was going to inquire when her baby was due.

Instead, Mary Kay had recognized Nancy as having attended several of the previous future Sales Directors meetings. "You've been here before, haven't you?

"I don't want you to be in this future Sales Directors group forever. You go home and give yourself a promotion."

Nancy knew what that meant, and although she may not have had the confidence to think she could succeed, Mary Kay's encouragement gave Nancy newfound courage. Her son was born in May and by August, Nancy had promoted herself to Sales Director.

"Her taking time to focus on me was just what I needed to get me over the hump," recalls Nancy.

As for the Cinderella lifestyle, Nancy has surely lived it. But she treasures most of all the time spent with Mary Kay Ash. "I've walked down cobblestone streets in Switzerland, arms locked with Mary Kay Ash. I've been in Mary Kay's hotel room when she had a jewelry designer display an entire collection, and we got to pick what we wanted. I was seated with Mary Kay at a London theatre production when one of the cast members came out to meet her. The young woman knelt down beside Mary Kay as Mary Kay took her hands and told her how great she was."

"Everywhere we go, we are treated like queens."

And in true Cinderella style, Nancy says, "Then we go home to the real world and feel very blessed that we have a career like Mary Kay, where a real woman can feel like a queen."

Shirley Metric

The Rule of Three Feet

*She's not sure what the planned topic
was that day for the speech, but she
did realize why there was a switch.*

Mary Kay always understood that women react to
criticism much more emotionally than men do. She taught
her Sales Directors that when they had a problem with an
individual in their unit, the best way to deal with it was to
educate the whole group. That way the person who needed
the coaching would pick up on it without personal
embarrassment.

Shirley Metric knew this lesson well that day as she scurried
to hear Mary Kay speak. She had spotted Mary Kay Ash the

moment she stepped onto the crowded elevator, but not wanting to bother her moments before she was to speak, Shirley moved to the back of the elevator and never said a word.

"I was seated with my friends by the time Mary Kay strode into the room. I could see the fire in her eyes," recalls Shirley.

As she began speaking about the rule of three feet (that is, speaking to everyone who comes within three feet of you), Shirley began sinking into her seat. Mary Kay said she couldn't imagine getting onto an elevator or an airplane without acknowledging the other people present. It was the first time Shirley had heard Mary Kay use what became a "pet phrase" of hers – "some women are all vogue on the outside but vague on the inside."

"I was mortified and truly ashamed of myself," Shirley says.

"I knew she was using the fact that I hadn't spoken to her on the elevator as a lesson!"

The worst part for Shirley was that Mary Kay stood at the door as everyone departed the meeting. "When I approached, she wrapped my arm under hers and whispered, 'Let's have lunch together.' I am positive that was her way of wrapping the criticism she'd just leveled at me in praise."

Shirley never forgot the lesson about being friendly to others. But more important, she saw firsthand how to, as she says, "demonstrate the charitable spirit; to have faith that even when people stumble, they can learn and grow."

Mona Butters

A Tale of Two Women

*The greatest thrill of growing
a career with Mary Kay is the
opportunity you have to touch and
change so many lives for the better.*

" We are like sifters. When I think of the *Paychecks of
the Heart*, I can't help but think of the many women who've
become a part of my life. The fact that I have been there to
witness firsthand their journey to success is one of my
greatest satisfactions," says Mona.

Two of her offspring Sales Directors come instantly to mind.

One started her Mary Kay business in the midst of a divorce filed by her husband. She was left with nothing. When Mona met her, Kym was struggling to make ends meet by teaching piano lessons in her home and battling years of demeaning, unkind words, which had left her beaten down.

Mona watched and encouraged as Kym emerged into a self-confident and outgoing woman. She learned everything she could about her career, worked diligently at her business and eventually earned the use of a pink Cadillac. Recently, Mona celebrated with Kym as she signed the mortgage to a new home she purchased on her own.

"What a beautiful progression from where she was to where she is," says Mona. "And what a tribute that she refused to be bitter or angry about her situation."

Another of Mona's Sales Directors also refused to be angry about what life had dealt her – she just went about doing everything she knew to change things. When she first started her business, Lyndell was barely scraping by.

One winter when Mona visited, she noticed Lyndell's trailer was so poorly insulated she had stuffed the cracks and holes with paper towels and tissue to keep out the cold winds. Still, the winds would howl. Another time, Mona watched as Lyndell crawled through the hatchback of her car to get to the driver's seat. Her door locks were frozen. The drafty trailer and the defective car were all she had, and she was determined to make the most of them.

"Lyndell grew up wearing hand-me-downs that had patches on top of patches in order to make ends meet. She told me that when she first began her Mary Kay business and heard talk of trips and diamonds, she couldn't relate at all to these prizes."

Today, Mona has proudly watched as the drafty trailer and the malfunctioning car have long since been replaced. "Today she can relate to trips and diamonds. Lyndell is sold on the Mary Kay dream because she has lived it."

My Story

Yours will be the 113th story.

*What cherished memory
or experience provided you
with the lesson that
money could never buy?*

My Story continued...

Acknowledgements

So many departments within Mary Kay touch any project of this magnitude. However, this book could not have been completed without the caring hands of:

Cynthia Pytlak, Tammy Proulx, Cindy Remington, Emma Jones and Kathy Boone who provided administrative support.

Peggy Meador, Peggy Anderson, Allyson McBride, Dora Hilburn, Marcelle Trammell and Erin Myers who proofread the contents.

Russ Mack, Kathy Albright, Kelly McIntyre-French, Bruce Mueller, Claudia Khan, Sandy Beaird and Jennifer Cook who lent their special expertise.

What a privilege the work has been for all of us as we honor our founder, Mary Kay Ash. One of our greatest "paychecks" is the knowledge that Mary Kay, a pioneer for women of the 20th century, will continue to influence and help women in the 21st century.

Yvonne Pendleton

About the Author

Yvonne Saliba Pendleton is a member of the staff at the world headquarters of Mary Kay Inc. in Dallas, Texas. An award-winning journalist by profession, she has worked closely with Mary Kay Ash. Since joining Mary Kay Inc. in 1991, she has written extensively about the National Sales Directors as well as many other members of the independent sales force. Yvonne is the author of the *From Our Hearts* collection, as well as the Mary Kay audiotape series, *Pearls of Wisdom*.

Prior to joining Mary Kay, Yvonne co-authored a history of Dallas, *Proud Heritage, Shining Future*. She has written for several national magazines. As an editor with the Times Mirror and Newhouse media organizations, she received awards from The Associated Press and United Press International among others.

Yvonne was runner-up for one of journalism's highest honors, the J. C. Penney/University of Missouri award. Named an outstanding journalism graduate of the University of Alabama, Yvonne recently profiled her own family for a Landmark Park exhibit on the founding families of Dothan, Alabama.

She and her husband are the parents of two children.

Index